THE

# PROGRESS OF PHILOSOPHY

## IN THE PAST AND IN THE FUTURE.

BY

SAMUEL TYLER, LL.D.

*Second Edition, Enlarged.*

"Whatever I write, as soon as I shall discover it not to be *truth*, my hand shall be forwardest to throw it into the fire."—LOCKE.

"The grandeur of man is to prefer what he believes to be truth, to himself."
COUSIN.

PHILADELPHIA:
J. B. LIPPINCOTT & CO.
LONDON: TRÜBNER & CO.
1868.

TO

# JOSEPH HENRY, LL.D.,

SECRETARY OF THE SMITHSONIAN INSTITUTION,

Who, while he has devoted his life with eminent success to the investigation and advancement of physical science, has always recognized the usefulness as well as the intellectual dignity of rational philosophy, this tract is appropriately inscribed by his friend the author.

FREDERICK CITY, MD., July, 1858.

# PREFACE.

In August, 1857, an eminent philosopher* of Europe in a letter to me said: "The position of America in many respects qualifies it admirably for the task of sifting the wheat from the chaff in the various conflicting philosophies of Europe, and producing from the materials of the older literature, aided by the independent spirit of her own thinkers, a system adapted to the character and wants of the age." It is to do something towards the development of such a system that I have prepared this tract. I have endeavoured to show that the true philosophy is founded upon an analysis of consciousness within the bounds of common sense. I have pursued this course of speculation from the beginning of the Greek epoch down to the present time, and have pointed out, both by positive and negative criticism, the one perennial doctrine advancing from age to age by new contributions, until it seems manifest, that its conflicts with other systems have only served to develop it into that complete doctrine which will be evolved by the discussions of the future directed in the same course, and reposing on the same foundation in the data of consciousness. I have, too, at appropriate points indicated what seems to me initials of new

---

* Mr. H. L. Mansel, of Oxford.

revelations in the one perennial evolution of philosophical truth.

This tract has been composed from two articles contributed by me to Reviews. The one, constituting the first part, was published in the Southern Quarterly Review for November, 1856. The other, constituting the second part, was published in the Princeton Review for October, 1855. The articles met with so much favour in Europe and America, that I am induced to publish them in this form. The article in the Princeton Review was read by Sir William Hamilton before his death, and he intended* to honour me with an answer to my dissenting criticisms, but death deprived us of the light which he doubtless would have shed upon the points in dispute. His forthcoming lectures will, perhaps, give us more light.

The foregoing remarks were the Preface to the first edition of this book.

I have added, to this edition, an article, published in the Princeton Review for January, 1862, which was called forth by Mr. Mansel's Limits of Religious Thought.

---

* Letter to me from Lady Hamilton.

# CONTENTS.

## PART FIRST.

### ANCIENT PERIOD.



### MEDIÆVAL PERIOD.



### MODERN PERIOD.



## PART SECOND.

### REACTIONARY EPOCH.

# PROGRESS OF PHILOSOPHY.

## Part First.

### THREE GREAT PERIODS.

THE relation of philosophy to its history is such, that the best mode of teaching it, even in system, if regard be had to its future as well as its past, is to exhibit it in its progress through its various aspects in the changing conditions of thought in the successive generations of men. By such a review, under the illumination of a criticism which throws over the doctrines of the earlier ages the light of the more mature doctrines of the later times, and brings forward to the later times, the various aspects which the problems presented to the struggling reason of the earlier ages, a fuller understanding of the doctrines of philosophy and of the problems both solved and unsolved may be attained. And the method of philosophizing, which science may have constructed, will receive confirmation and correction and expansion from the one perennial method which the endeavours both positive and negative of all sects of philosophers to explain, or to deny all explanation of, the phenomena of existence, will disclose as the rational tentative of universal reason striving for mastery over the unknown. By such a comprehensive survey, the narrowness of schools with their special points of view and their technicalities will be stepped over, and the basis of the one catholic philosophy will be discerned in those assumptions implicitly made, even in paradoxes, from the necessities of intelligence by all sects of philosophers; and on which as explicitly announced doctrine, the bewildered reason has, at last, been content to seek its rest. And upon this one catholic doctrine, can be grafted whatever of original thought we may have to contribute to the great tree of philosophy, at the parts of its growth where it most fitly pertains.

Such is the plan of this tract, as, in our judgment, especially suited to America where there are no schools of philosophy, but where a superstructure of our own is to be reared upon the foundations of European thought.

The progress of philosophy (overlooking the Eastern period anterior to that of Greece) presents three great periods: 1. Antiquity; 2. The Middle Ages; 3. Modern Times.

## ANCIENT PERIOD.

Ancient philosophy comprehends three epochs. The first, from Thales to Socrates, about one hundred and thirty years, gave rise to four principal sects—the Ionic, founded by Thales; the Italic, founded by Pythagoras; the Eleatic, founded by Xenophanes; and the Atomic, founded by Leucippus and Democritus. The second epoch was from Socrates to the promulgation of Christianity, about five centuries. The third epoch extends from the preaching of Christianity to the age of Charlemagne, or rather into the sixth century, for philosophy, like all other cultivation, was extinguished in the barbarism which immediately preceded the reign of that great monarch.

From Thales to Socrates, but one problem was discussed—the origin of existence; the essence of things; the formation of the universe. Each of the four sects of philosophers, during this epoch, was distinguished for the boldness of its hypothesis in attempting to account for the origin of the universe. The different sects varied from each other only in the principles of their solution of the one problem. The magnificence of the world without withdrew philosophers from contemplating the world within. Philosophy was, therefore, physical, not psychological—of nature, not of the mind. The contemplation of nature had filled the poets Hesiod and Homer with mythical dreams. Every part of the physical world had been personified by them. In their age, the Greek mind had no other notion of causation than the agency of actual personages. All the operations of nature were supposed to be carried on by the immediate agency of actual persons. The four sects of philosophers which we have mentioned, dispelled the myths of the poets from the contemplation of nature, and substituted for persons, powers or forces inherent in matter, as the causes or formative principles of nature. And Anaxagoras even suggested one Mind as the framer of all things. These four sects of philosophers made the first step in philosophy beyond the mythopoeic conceptions of the poets. In the poets, the emotional element of the mind was paramount, expending itself in a personifying sympathy, peopling the earth with all those personages which figure in Greek mythology. In the philosophers, the intellectual element was paramount, looking at the operations of nature as mechanical and dynamic. Still, the thoughts of the highest minds were directed to the contemplation of the panorama of the external world.

To the sects of philosophers which we have considered, succeeded the Sophists. This class of thinkers belongs to a peculiar stage in human progress—to a period of criticism or transition. The previous sects of philosophers had failed to find any platform of truth on which the reason of man could rest satisfied. Their labours had ended, and no fruits had been garnered into the treasury of knowledge. They, too, had no successors in their labour to solve the problem of the universe. The different views of nature, taken by the several sects, had all proved unsatisfactory, and yet seemed to have left no other possible view. This, the Sophists saw. The Sophists were, in truth, the offspring of the thinking of these sects of naturalists. Their parentage is shown in the fact, that, in general, they were materialists. The common doctrine of the Sophists was, that doubt attaches to every opinion, and that it is impossible to find certainty in anything. They were thorough skeptics. However much these actors in the great drama of thought may differ in special doctrines, on the one thing of skepticism they were agreed; and in their skepticism we find the place on which they stand in the great order in which the leaders of thought, at different epochs, are marshalled in the sequences of history. We must not, as has been so often done, regard this era as one only of decadence; for, while we repudiate the opinion of Mr. Grote, that the Sophists were as honest teachers as Socrates, and their doctrines only a little less enlightened, we readily admit that they planted in the field of thought many fruitful germs. They called out investigations in the theory of knowledge, in logic, and in language. The methodical treatment of many branches of knowledge was begun by them. They were the first to make style a special object of study amongst the Greeks. Greek rhetoric sprung out of their teachings. They, in a word, prepared instruments, and also cleared the way, to some extent, for the new progress which was to succeed.

Now begins the second epoch of ancient philosophy. Socrates is the leader in this period of the struggles of the mind of man with the difficulties of knowing theoretically—of construing to one's consciousness what he feels and sees within and without himself. The Sophists had withdrawn attention from nature, and the solutions of those problems which had engaged the first four sects of Greek philosophers, and had fixed attention on language in itself, and in its contents. They, in fact, began a revolution in the thinking of the nation. Socrates was trained in their discipline. He profited especially by the lectures of Prodicus and Anaxagoras. In fact, his method was that of the Sophists; and when he turned his assaults upon them, his victories were not due more to the greater truth which armed his doctrines, than to his greater skill in their own art of dialectics; but yet, we must carefully distinguish the Socratic from the Sophistical spirit of philosophizing. That of the Sophists was proud and boastful, as their very name σοφιςτοι, *wise-men*, indicates: that of Socrates was humble, as the name he adopted, φιλοσοφος, lover of wisdom, to distinguish himself and school from the Sophists, shows. And while the spirit of the Sophists was boastful, it was skeptical; but while that of Socrates was diffident, it was hopeful of certainty and truth. The fruitful germ which Socrates introduced into philosophy, was the problem of human consciousness. The mind was, in his philosophy, its own point of departure, and its principal object. With him began the new era in philosophy, where the inscription on the Delphic temple, "Know Thyself," became the watchword of philosophy. In consciousness Socrates found that basis of truth which the Sophists had failed to discover. They dwelt upon language and its contents, and as these contents were merely the factitious unities of popular and uncritical observations, much contradiction, as well as vagueness, would be found in the doctrines of all prevailing thought. Socrates, therefore, based his method upon consciousness, and, by what he called *intellectual midwifery*, unfolded truth from the minds of those with whom he conversed. This was the positive application of his method; and so far it was his own. But then, it must be borne in mind that Socrates merely taught men *how to philosophize*, and did not teach them *philosophy*, for he declared that he had none to teach. Through the negative application of his method he refuted the Sophists, by showing contradiction between their doctrines This, however, was but the common dialectical method of the Sophists themselves, of asking questions adroitly chosen for their logical relations to the doctrines in dispute, and making the answers obtained, the premises from which conclusions are deduced at variance with the doctrines of your antagonist, and yet consonant with his admissions in the answers to your questions. Socrates achieved his triumphs in the thinking of his age, by adding a new force to the method of the Sophists, which made it positive as well as negative, and that in the profoundest applications as well as in ordinary problems which lie more on the surface of knowledge.

Socrates had many followers, who, though they diverged much from each other in doctrines, all gave much attention to human consciousness, and continued the Socratic movement. Amongst these were the two greatest thinkers of antiquity, Plato and Aristotle.

Plato, like every other philosopher, saw that the great end of philosophy is to explain the phenomenal world, and especially the sensible universe. For it is this universe that, from his earliest infancy, presses without ceasing upon the attention of man. Nowhere else is this object of philosophy more distinctly displayed than in the writings of Plato. He wrote no systematic treatise of philosophy; but his philosophical doctrines are woven through his various dialogues, not so much for themselves as for a basis to his moral, political, and physical theories; in the Phædo, to prove the immortality of the soul; in the Republic, to sustain his ethical and political principles; in the Timæus, to explain and verify his physical theories. Plato's philosophy is but the life, the central principle, of his practical doctrines. Man, living and acting amidst mysteries, and himself the greatest mystery of all, was the great object of the philosophy of Plato. To explain man, and all that concerns him, either in the past, the present, and the future, was what Plato strove to do by his philosophy. He did not turn away from the realities of nature, and spend his life in unreal dreams, as those who talk so much about his mysticism, opine. It was the actual, passing before our senses and experienced in our consciousness, that he attempted to explain, and to found upon a basis of verity.

With this view of the scope and purpose of Plato's philosophy, let us inquire into the method by which he endeavoured to accomplish his ends.

Socrates, the master of Plato, was duly impressed with the weakness of the human mind, and felt how narrow are the limits of human knowledge. In fact, he circumscribed human knowledge within much narrower bounds than most of the great teachers of our race. Physical inquiries he entirely repudiated as beyond the comprehension of man. He was, in truth, rather a moralist and dialectician, than a philosopher in the sense of one addicted to the higher walks of speculation. And the vice of his method was the one common to the Greek philosophers, of taking for granted that the notions contained in common language are sufficiently accurate and expressive of realities for a basis of philosophy. This is sufficiently exemplified in the discussion reproduced by Plato in the Phædo. It is taken for granted, that the doctrine of the immortality of the soul is deducible from the common notions then entertained upon the topics out of which the argument is constructed. There is no attempt to evolve new principles out of the facts of consciousness; no effort to trace lines of original speculation through secrets of psychological manifestations; but all the proofs are deduced from the inaccurate notions embodied in the language of the times. The doctrine, that all acquired knowledge is but a reminiscence of what was learned in a prior state of existence, approaches nearer to an attempt at the evolution of a new principle by reflective analysis from psychological phenomena, than anything else in the dialogue; but this was doubtless a sophism of Plato's own, put into the mouth of Socrates, and is, after all, a shallow pretence resting upon mere assumption. The whole inquiry consists of assumptions and ratiocinations. There is no sifting of premises, no searching for principles amidst psychological facts manifested in self-consciousness; but the whole fabric rests upon the notions embodied in the language of the people. There is no designed attempt at any more accurate basis for the deduction of conclusions. Though he saw, as we have said, that consciousness is the criterion of truth.

The doctrine of Plato, as to the circle of human knowledge and the powers of the mind, differed widely from that of Socrates. Plato thought that no speculation is beyond the reach of the human mind. His was an ambitious philosophy. But we will show, that, like the speculations of the other Greek philosophers, his philosophy was founded upon popular notions and remnants of doctrine handed down, in loose traditions, from older speculators, who built upon the same superficial basis.

The fundamental doctrine of Plato's philosophy is, that there are real entities subsisting in the universe, corresponding to the general terms used in language; and that these general entities, called *ideas*, are the only proper objects of science: and that the method of philosophizing is to close the senses, and dwell in intellectual contemplation on these *ideas*, and to note their relations and combine them into propositions, and deduce conclusions from these propositions: and that the conclusions will correspond with the empirical truths of physics and the practical truths of morals, because the logical relations of these ideas correspond with the physical and moral relations of their images or representations—the phenomena of the physical and moral worlds. Such is the method of Plato when explicitly unfolded.

It results from such a method, that Plato's physics and Plato's logic, or, more strictly, Plato's metaphysics and Plato's dialectics, are the same. His physics is a logico-physics. The words of popular language embodied his whole field of observation. And the logical relations of the words, therefore, constituted, or were commuted with the physical relations of the things signified by them; because these things were nothing else than the popular meaning of these words. This is sufficiently exemplified in the Platonic doctrine of contraries. This doctrine is, that the ultimate powers of nature are contraries, and that everything is generated by its contrary. "There is (says Plato) a certain medium between the two contraries. There are two births, or processions—one of *this* from *that*, and of *that* from *this*. The medium between a greater and a less thing is increase and diminution. The same is the case of what we call mixing, separating, heating, evolving, and all other things without end. For, though it sometimes falls out, that we have not terms to express those changes and mediums, yet experience shows, that by an absolute necessity, things take rise from one another, and pass reciprocally from one to another through a medium." It is manifest, that the two *births*, or *processions*, spoken of as subsisting in nature between contraries, are nothing but the logical relations of the meaning of the words *greater* and *less*. There are no births, or processions, in nature, corresponding with these relations, constituting a generative medium between the entities *greater* and *less.* The whole doctrine is an affair of words. The reasoning is logico-physical. There is nothing real beyond the meaning of the words. The whole of philosophy and science is made nothing more than the development of the meaning of the terms of common language. Plato's philosophy, therefore, like all ancient philosophy, reposes upon mere popular notions. He finds the words, *equality, big, little,* and other like words, in popular language, and, instead of looking into nature for the real things intended to be signified by these terms, he conceives that there are realities independent of nature corresponding with them.

That Plato's supposed higher objects of knowledge, called *ideas,* are but the popular signification of general terms, is sufficiently manifest from Plato's own theory of the origin of this sort of knowledge. His theory is, that though the knowledge of *ideas* is acquired in a prior state of existence, yet it is recovered in this world by the ministry of the senses exercised upon individual objects, which recall the *ideas* by reminiscence. This theory shows that these *ideas* are but the general notions formed by every one in the exercise of his faculties upon the objects of nature. In other words, *ideas* are only the meaning of general terms, which express only relations, and afford no irrespective objects.

So, then, the Idealism of Plato, when sifted to the bottom, is found to be the mere Phenomenalism of the common mind—a lame empiricism. There is no deeper principle underlying it, as is pretended—no knowledge of higher essences remembered from a prior state of existence. A severe logic takes off the veil, and Plato is seen to stand on the common ground of the meagre empiricism of the ancient philosophy. All philosophers necessarily take their departure from the same general experiences, whatever may be pretended to the contrary; and the different results of their speculations will depend upon the difference in the accuracy, the extent, and the completeness of their observations, and legitimate inferences or deductions.

Aristotle appears next in Greek philosophy; he was the very genius of subtlety and of system; and no greater thinker has yet appeared in the family of man. He saw that the basis of science and philosophy must, from the very structure of the human mind, be phenomenal. Therefore he strove to fix logic on a psychological basis. With this view, he proceeded to analyze the senses, and account for the origin of knowledge through sensation. He repudiated the Platonic doctrine of *ideas*, and contended that the only real existences are individuals, and that generals *may* be nothing more, so far as the purpose of demonstration is concerned, than terms denoting a property common to an indefinite number of individuals. "The steady contemplation (says Aristotle, in his Metaphysics) of any individual object under that aspect in which it agrees with other individuals, will recall many similar objects to the mind; the stability of the one will communicate stability to the others, and thus give birth to what are called universals, that is, to general terms, equally applicable to an indefinite number of individuals." Laying down this doctrine as the basis of his theory of knowing, he at once constructed his logic in accordance with it. Therefore, in his Posterior Analytics, he thus lays down the psychological basis of demonstration: "For the purpose of demonstration, it is not necessary to suppose the existence of general ideas, but only that one general term can be applied with truth, and in the same sense, to many individuals. It is not necessary to suppose that general terms, denoting any class of substances, express anything besides the different particulars to which they apply, any more than the general terms denoting qualities, relations, or actions. One general term stands for a variety of particulars, considered under one and the same aspect; but to suppose that this term requires one substantial archetype or idea, as general as itself, is the hearer's fault; such a supposition not being necessary for the purpose of demonstration."

If we should stop our inquiry here, Aristotle would appear to be a mere Sensationalist; and such is, sometimes, the account of him in history. Plato is represented as a pure Idealist, while Aristotle is represented as a pure Sensationalist. This is a great mistake; each is both an Idealist and a Sensationalist—maintaining that human knowledge is derived from both the intellect and the senses. Plato, it is true, considers intellect exercised upon ideas, the sole source of *science;* yet he ascribed some degree of knowing to the senses. Aristotle ascribed much more importance to sense, but yet made both intellect and sense the conjunct principle of science. He rejected the Platonic doctrine of ideas, but, as we shall see, did not advance as far beyond it as the quotations from his writings which we have given above seem at first to indicate.

It behooves us here to inquire, what is the Platonic doctrine of ideas? The word *idea,* since the time of Des Cartes, has been employed to denote the objects of our consciousness in general; and, since the time of Gassendi and Condillac, whose school analyzed our highest faculties into our lowest, the word has been used to denote the objects of our senses in general. We have already seen that Plato used the word in a far different sense from either of these. He employed it to express the real forms of the intelligible world in lofty contrast with the images of the sensible. It was in this Platonic sense that Aristotle rejected the doctrine of ideas. "Plato (says Aristotle) came to the doctrine of ideas, because he was convinced of the truth of the Heraclitic view, which regards the sensible world as a ceaseless flowing and changing. His conclusion from this was, that if there be a science of anything, there must be, besides the sensible, other substances which have permanence; for there can be no science of the fleeting." In Plato's view, science demanded the reality of ideas as permanent existences, independent of sensible phenomena. Aristotle maintained that there is no proof of the independent reality of ideas; and that, at any rate, the doctrine furnishes no ground for the explanation of being. That Plato, in order to make science possible, had arbitrarily posited certain substances independent of the sensible and uninfluenced by changes—but that only individual things are offered to us objectively. Therefore, that it is the individual which is conceived as universal, or perhaps, that the universal is perceived in the individual; and that this conception or perception is the objectified idea of Plato.

The doctrine, that the universal can be perceived in the individual, which was, *perhaps*, the opinion of Aristotle, when sifted to the bottom, is simply this. The products of the understanding or generalizing faculty have both a general and an individual element, constituting two opposite logical poles. The simplest operation of this faculty is to compare together the points of resemblance between objects, and reduce them to one in the synthesis of thought. The product of this process is a concept. A concept being the result of a comparison, necessarily expresses a relation; it therefore affords no absolute or irrespective object of knowledge. In this aspect, it is general; but it can be realized in consciousness, by applying it, as the term of relation, to one or more of the objects which agree in the point or points of resemblance which it expresses. In this aspect, it is individual. A concept, therefore, is a synthesis of the universal and the individual expressed in a term of relation. And it is the obscure consciousness of this conjunction of the universal and the individual in the products of the understanding, which has led men to assert the existence of universals in nature. It is but the common error in philosophy of commuting the subjective for the objective. This criticism, we believe, has never been made before. It seems to us to furnish a clue to the fundamental errors in philosophy.*

From the criticism of Plato's doctrine of ideas, arose Aristotle's doctrine of matter and form. Aristotle

---

* It is the clue to the error that all knowledge must be through previous knowledge—that our cognition of a class or universal is prior to that of the individual. Though intuition must precede conception, yet the individual *as such* and the universal are discerned simultaneously. We cannot distinguish one individual from another without being conscious of the notion which that individual exemplifies. The general notion is necessarily conceived along with the individual which is discerned under it. This is possible, because things are presented in plurality, and conception must begin at once in aid of intuition to complete the apprehension of the individual.

enumerates four metaphysical causes or principles; *matter*, *form*, *moving cause*, and *end*. But these four can be resolved into the fundamental antithesis of matter and form. Matter and form, therefore, are, according to the Aristotelic doctrine, the only things which cannot be resolved into each other. Matter, according to Aristotle, is capable of the widest diversity of forms, but is itself without determinate form: it is everything in possibility, but nothing in actuality. Matter is thus a far more positive thing with Aristotle than with Plato, who treated it as a shadow. We must guard against the supposition, that Aristotle means by *form* what we mean by *shape*. The Aristotelic form is an activity which becomes actualized, through matter, in individual objects.

Aristotle's theory of knowledge corresponds with his theory of forms. As, according to his metaphysical doctrine, forms or universals exist not apart from, but in individual objects, he made, as we have said before, both intellect and sense important faculties in science. He held that there is an *a priori* knowledge paramount to, but not exclusive of, the *a posteriori*. That, though universals are known through the intellect and implicitly contain particulars, yet we may remain ignorant of particulars until they are realized through the senses. Therefore, that intellect and sense combine in framing the fabric of science. Accordingly Aristotle's method is two-fold, *deductive* and *inductive;* the first allied with intellect and forms or universals; the second, with sense and individuals. In conformity with this doctrine, Aristotle seems to have considered syllogism proper, or deduction, no less ampliative than induction; that deduction did, in some way, assure us, or fortify our assurance, of real truth.

Though Aristotle turned the mind to outward contemplation, he did not perceive the full import of observation, nor the full scope of induction. He still, in conformity with ancient thinking, made universals the paramount element of science, and intellect the paramount principle. It is true, that his doctrine of universals differed metaphysically from that of Plato; but logically it came to very much the same result in its influence upon method. There are, according to Aristotle's theory of knowledge, certain universal principles existing in the mind, rather as native generalities than as mere necessities of so thinking, which furnish the propositions for syllogism; therefore syllogism or deduction is not dependent for these on induction. Syllogism is thus the paramount process, and induction an inferior process, which may be used as corroborative of deduction; and may be especially used by such minds as cannot *a priori* realize universals, but may perceive them in individuals. Aristotle directed all his energies towards constructing a system of deductive logic. And he assumed that the notions contained in the language of his day were sufficiently accurate for philosophy and science. Some of the profoundest distinctions of his philosophy are to be found in the very structure of the Greek language. The distinction, for instance, of power into *active* and *passive* which is said to have been established by Aristotle, and was adopted by Locke and by Leibnitz, is found in the very fabric of the Greek language, which possesses two sets of potential adjectives, the one for active and the other for passive power. Those significant of active power are denoted by the termination ικος, and those of passive, by that of τος.* Though, therefore, Aristotle extricated logic from the metaphysical errors of Plato, he fell into a like error, but not so gross, under a different name; for Plato's *ideas* and Aristotle's *forms* are, at bottom, but the common notions expressed by general terms. In his investigations, Aristotle generally starts out by saying: "It is said so and so;" and his procedure is ratiocination founded upon common notions. The doctrine of contraries, too, as was the case with Plato, is a sophistry by which he deceived himself. And in his reasonings, his doctrine of *forms*, sometimes, unconsciously to himself, slips into Plato's doctrine of *ideas*. And we doubt whether Aristotle's estimate of induction, as a method of material inquiry, was higher than that of the ancient

* Ποιητικον signifies that which can make, and ποιητον, that which can be made; κινητικον, that which can move, and κινητον, that which can be moved.

Greek skeptics as recorded by Sextus Empiricus in these words: "Induction is the conclusion of the universal from individual things. But this induction can only be correct in as far as all the individual things agree with the universal. This universality must, therefore, be verified before its induction can be made: a single case to the contrary would destroy the truth of the induction." The weakness of induction, as indicated by this criticism of the skeptics, was overrated by Aristotle; as his whole logic seems to assume, in the very subordinate place given to induction. But yet Aristotle was so superior to all other Greek philosophers as an observer of nature, that we find in Suidas, he is called *the interpreter of nature*—'Αριστοτέλης τὴς φύσεως γραμματεὺς ἦν.

Let it not be supposed, from what we have said of the deficiencies of the Aristotelic logic, that we value it at a low estimate; it is far otherwise. We put the highest estimate, both upon the influence which it has exercised directly upon the progress of knowledge, and indirectly in disciplining the higher faculties of the mind. It was as great a need in Aristotle's time as the inductive method was in Bacon's. The work to be done, in the state of knowledge in Aristotle's time, was to sift the thought accumulated, discover its logical dependencies, eliminate, by the principle of contradiction, as Socrates did in his conversations with the Sophists, apparent errors, and retain what would stand the test of logical principles. The time had not arrived for the inductive method of objective observation and material illation. This we will endeavour to elucidate.

All thinking is either materially false, or formally false, or both. We have shown, that there was much material falseness in ancient philosophy; as the notions which formed its matter were the result of unscientific observation. But this was not the only vice of ancient philosophy. There was in it, also, a great deal of formal or logical falseness; and, until this was corrected, the time had not come for correcting its other vice. Even in so profound a thinker as Plato, there are paralogisms of every kind so gross as to astonish the modern mind not familiar with the looseness of ancient thought. The very ingenuity of the Greek mind led to sophisms. And many of these sophisms, which are seen by the modern mind to be a mere play of wit and acuteness, were deemed very important by some of the most distinguished thinkers of antiquity. In ancient times, men lived more in public, and carried on scientific investigations more in oral discussions, or conversations, than in the soliloquy of private meditation. Profundity, therefore, would be less valued than wit, dexterity in questioning, and adroit discovery of objections. The Sophists were accomplished masters in this art. There were, too, certain artificial rules, by which their dialogues were regulated. Every answer to a question, for instance, was to be *yes* or *no.* The interrogator, therefore, could constrain his adversary to move in a foreseen manner.

Now, as the method of science was not understood, men might perceive a fallacy, and yet not be able to point it out; for they had not even the requisite language to express these fallacies. How compendiously does the technical expression, "begging of the question," indicate a common fallacy! Such expressions, furnished by logic, not only facilitate the exposure of error, but enable us to get clearer views of truth. It was, therefore, the first demand of science, that the laws of thought should be investigated and understood, so that, by their application, fallacious reasonings might be discovered. This Aristotle attempted by considering the reasonings embodied in ancient thought. He saw that the clue to the whole scheme of Sophistry, was to discriminate the essence of the internal thought from the accident of the external expression. In this way he discovered that the syllogism is the one form of reasoning, and that fallacies consist in the covert violations of the logical laws which govern the syllogism. He developed this doctrine into the greatest monument of speculative genius which illustrates the history of philosophy. The great purpose of the Aristotelic logic, was to purge the understanding, and to keep it free of those errors which arise from the confusion and perplexity of inconsequent thinking.

The purpose of this tract forbids any more extended review of the doctrines of the followers of Socrates. Plato and Aristotle rise so far above all others in the importance of their contributions to the progress of philosophy, that, in a sketch like this, an examination of their doctrines must suffice.

The Romans were not acquainted with philosophy until after their conquest of Greece; and they never did succeed in speculative inquiries. Cicero reproduced and developed the moral philosophy of the Greeks, and, carrying the spirit of the orator into philosophy, he clothed it in the grand habiliments of the eloquence nurtured amid the meditative shades of Tusculum. "*Hanc enim perfectam philosophiam* (says Cicero), *semper judicavi quæ de maximis quæstionibus copiose posset ornateque dicere.*" But, for the most part, philosophy was at Rome degraded to a menial to serve personal interests, by displaying an apparent love of truth in a pretended devotion to elevated studies. Rome has, therefore, no contribution in the progress of philosophy.

After the Macedonian conquests, Alexandria became the great focus of learning. From its situation, it was the centre of the commerce of the world; many were attracted thither by the libraries of the Ptolemies. Here met philosophers from the East and the West; the religious dogmas of Jew and Gentile, Pagan and Christian, and systems the most opposing, met on the same arena. Plotinus, Proclus, and Porphyry, were the most distinguished philosophers of this school. Their doctrines were Platonic, and therefore the school was called Neoplatonic. Their philosophy was, however, a cloudy exhalation from the vast inundation of the confluent streams of diverse doctrines which had flooded in from many nations. It vanished before the light of Christianity. The only doctrines of Paganism, which existed after this period, were those adopted by the fathers of the Christian Church.

The fathers of the Church devoted little attention to philosophy, and still less to nature. They gave a preference to Plato, but were adherents of no particular system, culling and selecting from all. "God (says Chrysostom) did not send men into the world to syllogise and form arguments, but to expound the truth—not to dispute and contend with one another, but to deal out truth with impartiality. It was not in philosophical arguments that the Apostles interested themselves, but they preached simply and clearly, and it is from their example that we are to act." And Clement of Alexandria says: "What I call philosophy, is not what Plato and Aristotle have promulgated, but what they have spoken true and favorable to religion." Such are the most favorable views of philosophy entertained by the fathers of the Church. Some of the sects, especially the Epicureans and Stoics, they openly attacked. St. Augustine did more than any other of the fathers of the Church to further philosophy; but he conformed his doctrines to Christianity.

But this twilight of philosophy at last sunk into night in the sixth century, and for several ages there is a blank in the progress of speculation.

---

## MEDIÆVAL PERIOD.

Our modern philosophy, like our civilization, takes its rise in the middle ages. Its character in these ages, is philosophy under ecclesiastical authority—*philosophia ancillans theologiæ.* The middle ages begin when the Church became disencumbered from the ruins of ancient philosophy. This crisis was not until the time of Charlemagne. He was the vassal of the Pope. He opened schools throughout his vast empire; and from these philosophy obtained the name Scholastic. The clergy were the cultivators of this philosophy, and its character is given in the nature of its origin, and may be summed up in the saying of Joannus Scotus Eregina: *There are not two studies of philosophy and religion, but what is true philosophy is also true religion.*

The Scholastic philosophy is distributed into several epochs or changes. During the first, philosophy was under absolute subordination to religion; during the second, the subordination was softened down to an alliance; and in the third, a separation took place, indistinct at first, but finally more discriminating; and at last, terminating in modern philosophy.

The rampant spirit of physical inquiry in this age, is too prone to look back at the schoolmen as mere logical knight-errants, and their philosophy as logic run mad, because it did not advance physical science. Because the schoolmen, not perceiving the relativity of general terms, and that they afford no irrespective objects, wasted so much time in disputes about Nominalism and Realism; and not discriminating the primary and secondary qualities of matter, and therefore not perceiving that the words denoting the secondary qualities were ambiguously applied both to the knowing mind and the object known, disputed, whether fire is hot, sugar sweet, grass green, and other like questions; it has been concluded that all their discussions were idle disputes of mere words. And because they were subject in all their judgments to the Church, as recognized arbiter, it has been supposed that all the doctrines of the schoolmen were the blind opinions ordered by the unreasoned decrees of the ecclesiastical hierarchy. In these conclusions there is great error; for, with all the circumscription of the Church, there was ample scope left for the loftiest speculations. Though the authority of the Church was imperative when it issued its mandate, yet it left a large proportion of the problems of philosophical theology undetermined; and questions which, among Protestants, would cause a difference of sects, were decided in either alternative without impairing the orthodoxy of the parties. The fact is, that the faculties of the human mind were never more vigorously exerted (just as is the case with lawyers, though their discussions move, too, within the limits of authority), than during the middle ages by the schoolmen; though often on trivial questions, with trivial results, but often on important questions, with important results.

We are indebted to the schoolmen for much of the analysis which shows from the nature of the thing that the formal laws of thought are the adequate object-matter of logic. We are also indebted to them for the proper scientific definition of truth, as *the correspondence or agreement of a cognition or a cognitive act of thought with its object.* The schoolmen did also much towards fitting the modern languages for philosophical thinking. The great problem of philosophy is, to analyze the contents of our acts of knowledge or our cognitions, and discriminate what elements have been contributed by the knowing *subject* and by the *object* known. There must, therefore, be terms adequate to designate these correlative opposites, and discriminate the share each has in the total cognition. The exact distinction of *subject* and *object* was first made by the schoolmen. This distinction involves the whole science of mind; for this science is nothing more than the articulate discrimination of the subjective and the objective, in themselves and in their mutual relations. The two opposite nouns, *subject* and *object*, and the corresponding adjectives, *subjective* and *objective*, taken together and correlatively, enable us to designate the primary and most important antithesis of philosophy in the most precise and complete manner. Therefore it is seen that the most important seeds of modern philosophy are to be found in the Scholastic.

The capture of Constantinople by the Turks, in the year 1453, scattered over the West the learned Greeks of that capital; and then it was that philosophy rebelled against the supremacy of Aristotle and the Church. Philosophy, which had been the mere handmaid of the Church, came now to be cultivated for itself. New schools were opened, and almost every school of antiquity had its supporters. Europe beheld the revival of the Academy, the Lyceum, and the Porch. The system which first rose into greatest repute was the Platonic, contaminated with many mysteries of the Alexandrian fathers. But there arose a sect of independent thinkers, whose doctrines were subversive of even the spirituality of God and man. Cardanus, Telesius, Beregard, Cæsalpinus, and Vanani, present a group of philosophers who cannot be classed under any particular sect. They launched out into speculations which we are forced to admire for their vigour and independence. Skepticism had its supporters, at this time, in Montaigne and others. But the whole philosophy of this age was a mere reflex of that of antiquity. The want of method was the fundamental defect; and exclusive deference to authority was the great impediment to mental progress. It is difficult for us, in this age of free thought and speech, to realize the extreme submission to the authority of the Church, when that authority was exerted, and the absolute deference paid to Aristotle, during the scholastic period. The two great ends to be accomplished, in order to set free the human mind, were to discover a better method of philosophizing, and to shake off the yoke of authority.

---

## MODERN PERIOD.

Scholasticism had turned away the minds of thinkers from nature. But now, nature began to receive a remarkable degree of attention. The discovery of America, and of the passage to the East Indies, had widened the scope of view; and the discoveries of Copernicus, Kepler, and Galileo, had carried the thoughts of men beyond the limits of tradition and authority, and given an entirely new direction to the thinking of the age. These discoveries refuted a series of traditional errors and prejudices, and gave the thinking mind a self-dependence which caused it to break loose from the fetters of authority, and place itself upon the basis of observation and experiment, inquiry and proof.

At this juncture in the progress of thought, the most majestic and prophetic mind known to the history of philosophy, rose up to lead men in the new career of investigation which had been begun. Trained in the practice of a jurisprudence the most technical, and in its routine the most servile, and the most obedient to authority and traditional usage of any which has been established amongst men, we see the remarkable spectacle of a Lord Chancellor of England laying aside, for the moment, the king's seals, to become the keeper of the seals of nature. And in a majesty of diction unparalleled in the history of philosophy, this great thinker proclaimed to the world a new method of philosophizing to guide, the mighty spirit of inquiry which was abroad, over the fields of observation. Philosophy, no longer confined to the schools, is led forth by a politician and lawyer, out from the confines of authority into the amplitudes of nature. From this moment, the freedom of the human mind was established. This man of business, this accomplished courtier, this cunning lawyer, this consummate orator, this leader in the affairs of the world, appears on the stage of philosophical thought, with a more comprehensive grasp of thinking and a greater forecast, than any one of even the many trained especially to philosophy, who had preceded him. It is, at once, manifest to the eye of history, that a great revolution in the modes of philosophical thinking has been accomplished; and that henceforth philosophy is to pursue new paths. The power of the schools is gone, and that of the individual is asserted and established. Authority can no longer prevail against reason.

The revolution which Bacon effected is analogous to that accomplished by Socrates; for as the latter was said to bring down philosophy from heaven to earth, so the former may be said to have brought philosophy from books and tradition to nature. The philosophy of antiquity, Bacon showed, leaped at once to the highest generalizations or laws, without attending to those intervening particulars, through which we must pass to arrive at a perfect generalization. Its method was a treacherous logic, as we have shown, which limited everything to the mechanism of language; and as words serve only as registers of our thoughts, our doctrines cannot be exempt from error, unless we determine the original notions for ourselves. It is, therefore, says Bacon, necessary to purge the mind of these errors which it has imbibed. He therefore attempted, what was never attempted before, a systematic classification of the kinds of error. Of these he enumerates four, and calls them Idols. The first he calls Idols of the Tribe, being inherent in human nature; the second he calls Idols of the Den, being those of each individual; the third he calls Idols of the Market, being those formed from the society of men; the fourth he calls Idols of the Theatre, being false notions derived from systems of philosophy, and the contents of popular language. Bacon makes philosophy a mere interpretation of nature, and says: "The doctrine of idols bears the same relation to the interpretation of nature as that of the confutation of sophisms does to common logic." Therefore, the first step in a true method of philosophizing (interpreting nature) is to point out "the idols and false notions which have already preoccupied the human understanding, and are deeply rooted in it." The second step is, "the formation of notions and axioms on the foundation of true induction, which is the only fitting remedy by which we can ward off and expel these idols."

Bacon points out the difference between the ancient method and his own in these words: "There are and can exist but two ways of investigating and discovering truth. The one hurries on rapidly from the senses and particulars to the most general axioms; and from them as principles, and their supposed indisputable truth, derives and discovers the intermediate axioms.

This is the way now in use. The other constructs its axioms from the senses and particulars, by ascending continually and gradually, till it finally arrives at the most general axioms, which is the true but unattempted way."

It is important to have distinctly in mind the precise end which Bacon designed to accomplish by his new method, or Novum Organum. It was manifestly intended to supersede the old method, or Organon of Aristotle. Its very name evinces this. Much difficulty, however, has been created in regard to this question, by making distinctions in logic, which neither Aristotle nor Bacon understood. Logic has very properly come to be distinguished into pure and concrete or modified logic. Pure logic is conversant about the form of thought; concrete logic is conversant about the form of thought as modified by the empirical circumstances, external and internal, under which man exerts his faculties. Pure logic, therefore, proposes as its end, the *formal* or *logical* perfection of thought, and has nothing to do with its *real* truth, while the end of concrete logic is real or material truth. Now, it has been contended that Aristotle's logical treatises are of pure logic, while Bacon's treatise is of concrete logic; and that consequently their scopes are entirely different, and the ends intended to be accomplished by Aristotle and Bacon are different also. In this opinion there is some truth and much error. Aristotle had no definite, certainly no adequate, notion of the distinction between pure and concrete logic; and therefore has, throughout the logical treatises which have come down to us, confounded the two. The end of his logical treatises was not merely formal or logical truth, but real or material truth also; the two not, in fact, being discriminated. It was as a means towards real and material truth, that Bacon considered the Aristotelic logic; and it was in this aspect he designed to supersede it. The whole force of the Novum Organum rests upon this fact. The Aristotelic logic had in fact confounded the distinction between formal and material truth; and it was this very confusion which constituted its vice. In consequence of this confusion, it was considered a method of philosophizing, a means by which new truths could be elicited or gathered in. It was, in other words, considered creative, and not merely plastic. It is true, that Aristotle hangs the whole chain of our mediate knowledge upon a comprehensive belief, and maintains that the ultimate or primary principles of knowledge are incomprehensible, and rest in a blind, passive faith. Yet, such seems to have been his notion of the scope of syllogistic reasoning, that, somehow or other, as we have already said, he makes it independent of induction; and in this seems to ignore his principle of primary beliefs. At all events, he has left the relation and correlation of syllogism and induction so confused, and his psychological, metaphysical, and logical doctrines so ill adjusted, that we feel warranted in saying that Aristotle confounded formal and concrete logic, and formal and material truth. Bacon, therefore, viewing the Aristotelic logic as a method of philosophizing, of searching for material truth, attempted to supersede it in that purpose: but to leave it as a means of formal truth, of discussing questions about which there is no dispute as to the data. This was certainly Bacon's view and purpose. His whole doctrine of method is directed to the contents, and not to the form of thought—to the matter, and not to the consecution, of our thinking. It is from this point of view we must look at the Novum Organum to appreciate it.

The great fallacy which Bacon directed his hostility against, as the one which especially vitiated ancient philosophy, is the commutation of the subjective with the objective. All the errors which Bacon classified as Idols are subjective illusions, which had been commuted in the ancient philosophy with objective realities. This fallacy manifests itself in two ways. The one is to assume that the notions of things contained in common language are correct and complete interpretations of nature, and that the true mode of building up science is to analyze these notions, and combine them in their logical relations, because the logical relations of the notions will correspond with the real rela-

5

tions of their objects. The other way is to assume that there are general notions or principles, which are an original furniture of the mind, or are remembered from another state of existence, and that nature must conform in its manifestations to these ideas, and that by considering these ideas we can interpret nature. Both of these manifestations of this cardinal error are, as we have shown in our review of ancient philosophy, at bottom the same. That its true character is the commuting of the subjective with the objective, is manifest in the consideration, that as a notion is the joint product of the action of the subject and object, it follows that whatever a notion contains not corresponding with the object, must be the contribution of the thinking subject alone; and if the notion be only a partial interpretation of the object, but is considered complete, it is still mistaking an ideal illusion for a real object. The grand error of the ancient philosophy was to combine, and by syllogistic or deductive reasoning develop, these subjective illusions into systems supposed to be explanations of objective realities.

The whole scope and end of Bacon's method was, therefore, real or material truth. And here the question arises, *what is truth?* The schoolmen, as we have already shown, have given an answer which is now acquiesced in as correct. *Truth is the correspondence or agreement between our thought and its object—between our thought and what we think about.* The Baconian method was especially directed to maintain this view of truth. "For we are founding (says Bacon) a real model of the world in the understanding; such as it is found to be, not such as man's reason has distorted." Again he says: "We neither dedicate nor raise a capitol or pyramid to the pride of man, but rear a holy temple in his mind, on the model of the universe, which model we imitate." And still further: "Let men learn the difference that exists between the idols of the human mind and the ideas in the divine mind. The former are mere arbitrary abstractions; the latter, the true marks of the Creator on his creatures, as they are imprinted on and defined in matter by true and exquisite touches." It was, therefore, to the objective world that Bacon especially directed attention, so as to secure the mind from the vice of the ancient philosophy—of commuting the subjective with the objective—of substituting the fictions of the imagination for the realities of nature.

As, then, Bacon's method has in view the advancement of the real sciences, it may be well, for the sake of precision, to state what are the objects of these sciences, as, according to the view of truth above given, the correspondence between these sciences as systems of thought and their respective objects constitute their truth.

The real sciences are sciences of fact; for the point of departure from which they set out is always a fact, a presentation of mind. Some of these rest upon the presentations of self-consciousness, and these are facts of mind. Others rest upon presentations of sensitive perception, and these are facts of nature. The former are the mental sciences; the latter are the natural sciences. The facts of mind are given partly as contingent and partly as necessary. The latter, the necessary, are universal virtually and in themselves; the former only obtain a factitious universality by a process of generalization. The facts of nature, whether necessary in themselves or not, are given to us only as contingent and isolated phenomena, and therefore have only that empirical generality which we bestow on them by classification.

Now, it is with the facts of nature that Bacon's method, as developed by himself, more especially deals. The great end of his Novum Organum, therefore, is to ascertain that empirical generality, or factitious universality, amongst isolated phenomena of nature, which is accomplished by classification; for it is only in this way, according to Bacon, that man can bring the immensity of nature within the scope of his knowledge.

In accordance with this view of philosophy, particulars or individuals become the important objects of consideration in the Baconian method. And Bacon, in the face of ancient philosophy, which busied itself about universals, had to defend the study of particulars in these words: "With regard to the meanness or even filthiness, of particulars, for which (as Pliny observed) an apology is requisite, such subjects are no less worthy of admission into natural history than the most magnificent and costly; nor do they at all pollute natural history, for the sun enters alike the palace and the privy, and is not thereby polluted. For that which is deserving of existence is deserving of knowledge, the image of existence."

As, then, particulars are the primary objects of the Baconian method, this method must begin with the senses. Accordingly, Bacon says: "We must guide our steps by a clue, and the whole path, from the very first perceptions of our senses, must be secured by a determined method." And he enounces his method in these words: "It ought to be eternally resolved and settled, that the understanding cannot decide otherwise than by induction, and a legitimate form of it."

Here the question emerges, *what is induction?* Bacon had not a very discriminate notion of it. In the procedure which he calls induction, or rather by which he exemplifies it, he confuses analysis and synthesis, and does not even sufficiently discriminate between observation and induction; as he includes, in what he calls induction, the objective process of investigating individual facts as preparatory to illation, as well as the illation from the singular to the universal. Nor has any writer, as far as we know, sufficiently explained and exemplified induction. The loosest notions are entertained on the subject. By the best writers, induction is said to be analytical, whereas it is synthetical. This confusion, however, often arises from the confused and even contradictory notions which are entertained of analysis and synthesis. The process, which by some is called analysis, is called synthesis by others, and *vice versa*. These discrepancies and contradictions we will endeavour to explain, and found upon the explanation a more accurate determination of induction.

There is and can be but one method in philosophy; and what have been called the different and more or less perfect methods, are merely different applications of this one method to the objects of knowledge. Method is a rational progress—a progress of the mind towards an end; and method in philosophy signifies the progress conducive to the end which philosophy proposes. The ends of philosophy are two—the first being the discovery of causes; and the second, the resolution of things into unity. These ends, however, fall into one; as the higher we ascend in the discovery of causes, we approximate the nearer to unity. The detection of the one in the many is, therefore, the end to which philosophy tends continually to approximate. What the method in philosophy is, will appear the more clearly, if, in the first place, we consider philosophy in relation to its first end—the discovery of causes.

Causes,* taking the name for a synonym of that without which their effect would not be—and they are only coefficient elements of their effect; and effect is the combination of these primary elements to which we give the name of causes, and the concurrence of which gives existence to the effect. The acid and the alkali, for example, are the causes of the neutral salt, and also its coefficient elements. To the elements we give the name causes; to the combination, we give the name effect. Now, as it is by experience we discover what causes are necessary for the production of an effect, it follows that the only way by which we can attain to the knowledge of causes, as causes, is in and through their effect; and the only way we can become aware of their effect, as effect, is in and through its causes. In as far, therefore, as philosophy is the research of causes, the only necessary condition of the possibility of philosophy is decomposition. The decomposition of effects into their causes is called analysis. In its philosophical signification it means the separation of the parts of any complex whole.

But, though analysis is the fundamental process, it

---

* The *metaphysical* doctrine of causation is considered in the second part of this tract.

is not the only one. We analyze only that we may comprehend the objects; and we can comprehend only as we are able to reconstruct, in thought, if not in reality, what has been decomposed. This mental reconstruction is, therefore, the final procedure in philosophy, and is called synthesis. Of these two processes, the former is called the regressive, as ascending from effects to causes; the latter is called the progressive, as descending from causes to effects. These two processes are the necessary parts of one method, and are relative and correlative of each other. Analysis, without synthesis, is only a begun knowledge. Synthesis, without analysis, is no knowledge at all; for synthesis receives from analysis whatever elements it recomposes. Synthesis supposes analysis as the prerequisite of its existence, and is dependent on it for the qualities of its existence; for the value of every synthesis depends on the value of the foregone analysis. If the elements furnished by analysis be assumed, or not really discovered, the synthesis will, at best, be but a conjectural theory; and if the analysis be false, so will be the synthesis. The legitimacy of every synthesis, therefore, depends on the legitimacy of the analysis which it presupposes. These two relative procedures are thus equally necessary to each other in the acquisition of knowledge, and are as indispensable to the existence of philosophy as the processes of inspiration and expiration are to animal life. It is, however, to analysis that the pre-eminence is due, if to either; for though it be only a commencement, yet it is the preferable, inasmuch as it lays the foundation for synthesis; whereas synthesis without analysis is radically void.

As regards, therefore, the first end of philosophy—the discovery of causes—there is only one possible method, of which analysis is the foundation, and synthesis the completion.

Considering philosophy in relation to its second end—the resolution of our knowledge into unity—the same doctrine is equally apparent. Everything presented to our consideration in the external or internal world—whether through the medium of sense, or of self-consciousness—is presented in complexity. The senses present objects in multitudes, in each of which there is a congeries of many various qualities; and the same holds true of the presentations of self-consciousness, since every modification of mind is a complex state, and the different elements of each state manifest themselves in and through each other. Thus there is nothing but multiplicity presented to us. And our faculties are so limited, that they are able to take in only one object or combination, and that the very simplest, at a time. It is therefore only by analysis and synthesis that multiplicity can be brought into unity. In fact, the search for a cause, and the search for unity in cases where the notion of cause does not enter, are both governed by the same regulative principle—the principle or law of identity in its empirical application —as we shall show presently.

We see, then, that in any actual investigation, analysis and synthesis are necessarily used interdependently and interchangeably. They cannot be separated; and the two together make up the one method of philosophy. This method, according to Bacon, is observation and induction. As, then, analysis and synthesis constitute the one method, and observation and induction constitute it also, it behooves us to correlate analysis and synthesis with observation and induction. Before, however, we do this, let us give an articulate discrimination between observation and induction.

There are two ways by which we may become acquainted with things. In the first place, we may know a thing as simply existing. This is the knowledge of what simply is—of facts known in our own experience or that of others—and is called empirical or historical knowledge; for history is properly only the narration of a consecutive series of phenomena in time. It comprises all that information which we obtain from the physical world by sense, and from the mental world by self-consciousness. The process by which this degree or sort of knowledge is obtained, is what Bacon means by observation; and it manifestly involves both analysis and synthesis. The knowledge obtained in this way is, however, not philosophy. It requires another process to elevate it to that dignity.

Let us then consider the second way by which we may know things. The mind is so constituted, that it cannot perceive the existence of anything without referring it to something else as its cause, and without which it could not have existed. Things do not occur isolated from each other. There is no phenomenon but is the effect of some cause. Thus, when we see a rainbow, we may, in a certain sense, be said to know it; but with such knowledge, the mind does not rest satisfied; and it is only when we discover that the phenomenon depends on the reflection and refraction of light, by the rain falling from a cloud opposite the sun, that we can be said fully to know it. This is done by inferring from the analogies that the reflection and refraction of light is the cause, and then by mathematical reasoning deducing from the known laws of reflection and refraction, the breadth of the colored arch, the diameter of the circle of which it is part, and the relation of the latter to the place of the spectator and of the sun, and finding all these to come out of the calculus just as they are observed in nature. This knowledge of the cause of a phenomenon is something more than that phenomenon considered simply as a fact, and constitutes the second way in which we may be said to know anything, and is called philosophical, scientific, or rational knowledge—the knowledge of effects, as dependent on their causes. Now, into the procedure of acquiring this sort or degree of knowledge, induction as well as observation enters. The process by which the reflection and refraction of light are inferred or assigned as the cause of the rainbow, is induction, and is synthetic; for it brings the phenomenon of the rainbow under the laws of light—binds it with other phenomena of the same sort—is an illation from an individual or particular to a class, from a singular to a universal. It is seen, and we selected it for that reason, that in the instance given, induction is aided by mathematical deduction, but only *aided* by it; for the illation is purely inductive, and is assumed as true in the mathematical deduction, and only verified or confirmed by it; for mathematics does not take the physical sciences out of the pale of induction, but only aids induction. That induction is synthetic, all the discoveries in science show. From our limited experience that some bodies gravitate, we infer that all bodies gravitate. Here the mind binds up the several facts of observation into a whole—as it were, reconstructs an analysis; this is certainly synthetic. Induction is therefore clearly synthetic, and not analytic, as it has sometimes been said to be. It has sometimes been called both analytic and synthetic, especially by the mathematical physicists. When the procedure is from effects to causes it is called analytic, but when the procedure is from an ascertained cause to the explanation, by it, of analogous or resembling phenomena or effects, it is called synthetic. These procedures correspond with Bacon's, or rather are Bacon's ascending and descending scales of induction. This nomenclature is adopted, because the last procedure, which is also called deductive, is apparently the reverse of the first —the mere retracing of the same steps from the cause back to the same effects from which it was inferred; whereas other effects, analogous to those from which the cause has been inferred, are attempted to be brought within the same cause and explained by it. As the first process is called analytic, this is called synthetic. But at bottom both are synthetic, as they are both induction viewed from opposite points.*

It is seen, then, that method, in its universality, consists of two processes, analysis and synthesis, which are relative to, and complementary of, each other.

As philosophy has only one possible method, so the history of philosophy only shows the more or less imperfect application of this one method. It presents many aberrations *in* the method, but none *from* it. There never has been an attempt at philosophy where analysis and synthesis were not both used. But sometimes the one, and sometimes the other, has predominated; they have not been kept in due correlation in

* It should be remarked, that the terms analysis and synthesis, which have been derived from the mathematicians, are sometimes reversed; the first being applied, by some, to the process to which the latter is applied by others; and *vice versa.* But this is not the occasion to explain this confusion.

their employment. The ancient philosophy is especially defective, by the meagre employment of analysis. The analysis of phenomena was partial, and the synthesis consequently one-sided, and erroneous. The analysis of the early Greek physical philosophers, of whom we have spoken, who, fixing upon one or more elements as superior to all others, such as water or air, was partial; and consequently the synthesis, that it was the principle of all things, was one-sided and erroneous. Bacon has exhibited the deficiency of the physics of Aristotle in analysis, when he says: "Nor is much stress to be laid on his frequent recourse to experiment, in his books on animals, his problems and other treatises; for he had already decided, *without having properly consulted experience as the basis of decisions and axioms;* and, after having so decided, he drags experiment along as a captive constrained to accommodate herself to his decisions." And of the empiric school, as he calls it, he says, their dogmas are founded "in the confined obscurity of a few experiments." We have, in our review of ancient philosophy, shown that it was founded on the crude analysis contained in the language of the people. The great precept of the Baconian method is: *Do not hurry to a synthetic induction from an imperfect analysis, a narrow observation; but let your analysis be complete.*

Here emerges the question, *how are we to observe?*

In order to scientific knowledge, as we have described it, observation must become or turn into inquiry. We must question nature; but a question implies some knowledge of the thing inquired about. How, then, are we to inquire of nature, unless we have some intimation of her secrets—the human mind having no *a priori* clue to them? The questions put to nature must, too, be particular or leading questions.

The questioning of nature springs out of observation, by nature herself disclosing to us some clue to the secret. When we observe a certain correspondence among a number of objects or phenomena, we are determined by a principle of our intellectual nature to suppose the existence of a more extensive correspondence than experience has disclosed, or perhaps may ever disclose. This judgment, that where much is found accordant, all will be found accordant, is the result of an original tendency of our nature. It is the inventive principle by which we generalize our knowledge. This judgment is first only hypothetical—merely an *inventive principle*, which prompts us to put questions to nature, based upon the supposed truth of the judgment, and is called hypothesis. The actual procedure of philosophizing, therefore, consists of: 1. Observation; 2. Hypothesis; 3. Questioning; 4. Induction. This questioning is sometimes only the observation of the ordinary course of nature. Sometimes it is experiment; for, says Bacon, "the secrets of nature betray themselves more readily when tormented by art, than when left to their own course." If the answers accord with the first inference—the hypothesis which prompted us to put the questions—it is then assumed as verified, and the induction is complete. How many answers concurring to the same point amount to proof in any case, is beyond the determination of any rule. In some cases, a few instances warrant an induction; in others, an immense number are required to warrant the judgment. This difference results from the fact, that where the character inquired about is an essential one, like the lungs in a terrestrial animal, a few instances will suffice; but when the character is a contingent one, like the colour of things, hardly any number of instances will suffice. And whether a character is an essential or a contingent one, is itself a question of science, and must be determined before it can be used as a principle of evidence in induction.

The presumption, that where much is found accordant, all will be found accordant, has been considered by philosophers to be of two kinds—to be either induction or analogy. This seems to us to be erroneous. Though induction and analogy are to be distinguished, they are not to be distinguished as only relatives of one kind; they are not to be considered as two processes of reasoning; but induction is to be considered as the process, and analogy as the objective law warranting the process. In this view of the subject, induction may be defined *a material illation of the universal from the singular, warranted either by the general analogies of nature, or by the special analogies of the object-matter of any real science.* The synthetic inference is not necessitated by a law of thought, but only warranted by the observed analogies which merely incline the judgment. It seems to us, therefore, more accurate to make induction signify the *process*, and analogy or similarity signify the *evidence* on which it is founded; for such is the true account of the process, as the definition just given indicates.

In the inductive process, the conclusion is always wider than the premises. Whereas, in strict demonstration, no conclusion can contain more than the premises. In the inductive process, experience says, *this, that,* and the *other* body gravitate, and the conclusion says, *all bodies* gravitate. In explanation of this, it has been said, that the mind adds something of its own, warranting us to draw the conclusion. That the affirmation, *this, that,* and the *other* bodies gravitate, is connected to the conclusion, *all* bodies gravitate, by inserting between the two another proposition, to wit: *the supposition of the uniformity of nature.* And that as this supposition is not the product of induction, it must be interpolated into all inductive reasoning by the mind. And that, therefore, where the reasoning in induction is fully expressed, it will stand thus: *this, that,* and the *other* body gravitate; but as nature is uniform in all her operations, *this, that,* and the *other* body represent all bodies: therefore, all bodies gravitate.

Though this is the most scientific explanation which has yet been given by any philosopher, we feel constrained to demur to it; as, to us, it involves a concealed error. The affirmation of the uniformity of nature, which seems to be interpolated in inductive reasoning, can be resolved into something simpler, which makes the process accord with the great mental law, *that thought is always under the antithesis of subject and object; and that in the products or conclusions of thought, nothing is contained as objective which was not objective in the process of thinking.* In other words, the laws of intelligence never warrant an illusive interpolation of the objective for the subjective, as it must do if the uniformity of nature is predicated in the inductive illation. The veracity of human consciousness would certainly seem to require this view—otherwise the mind practises illusions upon itself, under the truest conformity to its own laws. We think this supposed uniformity of nature may be resolved into identity objectively perceived in nature. Thus, the principle of uniformity will thereby be resolved into the law of identity. This we will now show.

There are but three ultimate laws of intelligence: 1. The law of Identity; 2. The law of Contradiction; 3. The law of Excluded Middle; and a corollary from these, the law of Reason and Consequent. Now, reason, whether exerted in deductive or inductive (in apodictic or hypothetical) judgments, must always be regulated by the same laws. In other words, the laws of thought are the same in the deductive and the inductive processes; only that in the deductive (apodictic) they are absolute, and in the inductive (hypothetical) they are modified by empirical circumstances. The laws of thought alone determine the deductive process, necessitating the conclusion; but the laws of thought, modified by the analogies of nature, determine the inductive process inclining the judgment. In the inductive process, the laws of thought have an empirical application. And the law of identity is the special one which is gratified in the synthetic illation* by which the analogies are unified into identity. Objects which determine undistinguishable impressions upon us, are perceived and represented in the same mental modification, and are subjectively to us precisely as if they were objectively identical. When, therefore, a number of objects or phenomena are found

---

* The application of the law of identity explains synthetic judgments without resort to the complex, operose, and absurd assumptions of Kant, which only confuse and pervert the true doctrine.

to possess absolute similarity, and their difference is for the time lost sight of, their similarity is converted into identity, and they are thereby reduced into the unity of thought. By the same regulative law, similar phenomena are referred to an identical cause. Analogies or similarities are the footprints of identity. And what has been supposed to be the assumption of the uniformity of nature in every induction, is but identity, which the mind affirms upon viewing the analogies or similarities; for whatever is identical to consciousness, is so uniformly or universally. It is not, therefore, necessary to a theoretical explanation of induction, to assume, as a superficial analysis seems to warrant, that the uniformity of nature is affirmed as the major premise, which the mind, from the necessity of so thinking, interpolates in the reasoning. The mind considers no such principle. It affirms only what it perceives objectively—identity in similarity. Some water-fowl have web-feet—not by the assumption of the uniformity of nature, but by the law of identity—leads the mind to affirm that all water-fowl have web-feet. It is as though the mind had viewed all water-fowl. The inductive inference is, in fact, a sort of reaffirmation or repetition of what has been actually observed. If such were not the result of the guidance of the law of identity on viewing analogies or similarities, the mind would contradict itself—not think at all. For affirmation and negation are the ultimate alternatives of thought. Therefore, the law of contradiction combines with the law of identity, of which, in fact, it is a phase, in leading to the inductive synthesis or totalizing result.*

The error which we have thus endeavoured to expose by a more thorough analysis, results from the covert assumption, that syllogistic is the only reasoning; and that every general assumption which can be found, by reflective analysis, to be the condition of a product of the mind, must have been realized in consciousness as connate with the product at the time of the genesis of such product. For example: as the notion of space is found by reflective analysis to be the condition of the notion of body, it is supposed that the notion was natively latent in the mind, and was elicited into consciousness in the process of cognizing an external object; whereas, space or extension is cognized objectively as a necessary element of body, and must be realized in the cognition, as contributed by the object and not by the subject. The human mind is still fettered in philosophical thinking, by the ancient

* The apparent paradox of identity in diversity constituted one of the earliest puzzles in metaphysics; and gave origin to a skepticism which denied the possibility of uniting two notions in a judgment, which, of course, contravened the validity of the law of identity. Any objection to our explanation of empirical thinking under the law of identity, will be only a revival of the old skepticism which objected to the apparent paradox in the law of identity even in formal thinking or deduction.

doctrine of universals, and that all knowledge is through previous knowledge, and based on generals, which it was the great purpose of Bacon's philosophy to overthrow, and to emancipate the human mind to the full freedom of a philosophy of observation of individual phenomena.

As hypothesis is the great inventive principle of induction, by which, as we have already indicated, the questioning of nature is conducted, it demands articulate exposition. It is in the form of hypothesis that the grand heresy of commuting the subjective with the objective creeps into philosophy and science. Hypothesis is the initial ball, which is rolled through the field of observation, accumulating only what accords with it, so that the whole aggregation will be of the same character with the nucleus; and if what is first set in motion be erroneous, so will all that is accumulated. In order, then, to prevent the commutation of the subjective with the objective, it is necessary that the hypothetical supposition shall be an inference from phenomena, as it always is, in that which we have described as the normal procedure of induction. The supposition or provisional judgment arises upon the observation of phenomena, and guides our questioning of similar phenomena. But the great danger is, that our provisional judgment be the mere application of a pre-conception, like the vortices of Des Cartes in explanation of the motions of the heavenly bodies.

When a phenomenon is presented to us which we can explain by no causes within the sphere of our experience, we endeavour to recall the outstanding phenomenon to unity, by ascribing it to some cause or class to which there is a probability of its belonging. The great maxim, regulative of this procedure, is called the Law of Parcemony, and is adequately expressed by Sir William Hamilton in these words : "Neither more nor more onerous causes are to be assumed than are necessary to account for the phenomena." In commenting on this rule, which had been enounced by Newton, Sir William says, it is almost certain that Newton, when he says we are to admit no causes but such as are true (*veræ*), he meant "to denounce the postulation of hypothetical facts as media of hypothetical explanation." Now, it is not only *almost* but absolutely certain, that this was Newton's meaning: because he explicitly says so in the general scholium at the end of his Principia: "I have not been able (says he) to discover the cause of these properties of gravity from phenomena, and I frame no hypotheses: for whatever is not deduced from phenomena is called hypothesis; and hypotheses, whether metaphysical or physical, whether of qualities or mechanical, have no place in experimental philosophy. In this philosophy, particular propositions are inferred from phenomena, and afterwards rendered general by induction." Here Newton makes *cause* the opposite of hypothesis, and astricts hypothesis to mere assumptions not deduced from phenomena. He therefore means by *true* causes *real* causes—the opposite of supposititious causes. And the Principia is an exemplification of it; for amidst all the intricacies of mathematical demonstration, Newton, with the most marvellous caution and sagacity, never for a moment loses sight of phenomena and known causes. Induction is the centre and the circumference around and within which the mathematical demonstrations revolve. Newton's rule about true causes does not, as Dr. Whewell and others suppose, reject the inquiry into new causes. In the questions which Newton was considering, the true cause was the first term, the one which should be known, and not the second, the one unknown, as it always is, in a search for new causes. It would be illegitimate, according to Newton, to assign a subtle ether as the cause of the retardation of the planetary motions, as its existence is not known; but it would be perfectly legitimate as a *provisional judgment,* to infer the existence of a subtle ether from the retardation of the planets in their orbits. It was legitimate, to infer the existence of Leverrier's planet, as the cause of the perturbations in Uranus, as a *provisional judgment,* to be verified by subsequent observation, as was done; but to account for the perturbations by the existence of the planet, would be reversing the order, placing the unknown term first in the inquiry, and accounting for the known by the unknown.

Such is the comprehensive and profound method—sweeping as it does through all the intricacies of the heights and depths of nature — which Bacon proclaimed in his Novum Organum. "Although (says Newton, in his Optics) the arguing from experiments and observations, by induction, be no demonstration of general conclusions, yet it is the best way of arguing which the nature of things admits of." And the marvels accomplished by this method in unravelling the secrets of nature, have long since vindicated it from the objections of the ancient Greek skeptics, which we noticed in treating of ancient philosophy.

Des Cartes comes next in the history of philosophy. He was contemporary with Bacon, but thirty years younger. The influence for truth of no philosopher has, in our opinion, been more overrated. It is, therefore, time that his philosophy should be weighed in the scales of criticism, and its true value fixed in the progress of philosophy.

From the manner in which our opinions are formed, amidst the circumstances of life, our supposed knowledge cannot but be a medley of truths and errors. It is therefore important to institute a critical examination of the constituents of this knowledge. Des Cartes proposed that we should commence the examination by doubting all our opinions. Now, this initial or preliminary doubt of Des Cartes has always seemed to us, as a practical rule, extremely idle. For, let it be observed, this preliminary doubt is to be the forerunner of any system of truth. The whole contents of the mind are to be condemned until their truth is established. But how are we to begin the examination of our judgments? Not at random, of course, but by selecting them according to some principle, and arranging them in some order and dependence. But the distribution of things into their classes is one of the most difficult tasks of philosophy, as well as one of the last that are accomplished. Amongst our opinions there are many which can only be tested by profound investigation and extensive knowledge. This precept of Des Cartes, which is intended to show how we are to begin to be a philosopher, requires us to be one before we begin. The true precept, therefore, is not the unconditional one of absolute preliminary doubt, as Des Cartes teaches, but a gradual and progressive reprehension of prejudice. We should examine all our opinions with the circumspection which merely supposes that they contain some truth combined with much error. All, therefore, of value in the preliminary doubt of Des Cartes is, that it ignores authority. It implies that the judgments bequeathed to us shall not be decided by authority, but by a principle superior to authority within the sphere of truth—the principle of free thought acting within the limits prescribed by its own laws, and not subordinated to authority, and by it astricted to deduce conclusions from such principles as authority has admitted or ordained. But all this had before been articulately proclaimed by Bacon in the Novum Organum, in his masterly criticisms of the previous systems of philosophy, which he closes in these words: "Here, too, we should close the demolishing branch of our Instauration, which is comprised in three confutations: 1. The confutation of natural human reason left to itself; 2. The confutation of demonstration; 3. The confutation of theories or received systems of philosophy and doctrines." So that, at most, the preliminary doubt of Des Cartes is but a crumb dropped from the critical doctrines of Bacon.

This doubt of Des Cartes was a preliminary to the establishment of a system of positive doctrine; for Des Cartes was anything than a skeptic. Indeed, he hastened to his conclusions; and, as D'Alembert said, "began with doubting everything, and ended in believing that he had left nothing unexplained."

How, then, did Des Cartes essay to lay the foundation of knowledge? By reflection, he finds a basis for certainty in the fact of thought itself; in the fact of the very doubt that perplexes him. For, to doubt is to exist; therefore, the doubt reveals in consciousness both thinking and existence. This fundamental truth Des Cartes thus expressed: *Cogito, ergo sum.* Thus far, his philosophy is purely subjective. As yet, the operations of his mind—his mere thinking implying his existence—is all that he can hold true. Like all modern philosophers prior to Reid, he held that the mind possesses no immediate knowledge of anything but its own modifications, which the mind mistakes for external reality. How then, inquires Des Cartes, can it be known that external things exist, when the mind has no immediate knowledge of their existence? Des Cartes must, *ex hypothesi*, find in the mind itself some media of proof for external existence. Searching, therefore, in his mind, he finds the idea of God—a perfect intelligence, eternal, infinite—necessary. This idea, he argues, must have an adequate cause, which can only be a corresponding being; for it cannot be the product of the finite mind. Having thus established the existence of God, he deduces therefrom the existence of the outward world. If God be veracious, he argues, it follows that he who is the author of the sensible existences, is the author of the appearances which induce us to believe their existence, and that he would not exhibit these appearances as a snare and illusion; consequently what appears to exist does exist, and God himself is the guarantor that it is no illusion.

Now, this argument is wholly invalid. Indeed, it proves that God is the author of illusion. It cannot be denied, that we believe that the very objects which we perceive exist; and not that there is something representative of them which alone is perceived, and suggests their existence. We believe in the existence of things because we believe that we know them as existing. Now, Des Cartes, by his own theory, was deceived in the belief that we see things existing. God, therefore, is the author of illusion; and if the author of this deception, the conclusion is the very reverse of that drawn by Des Cartes. But his reasoning involves a further fallacy. It assumes, that God is veracious. How is this known? It can only be known by our faculties of knowing. But the argument assumes that our faculties are not trustworthy, because we believe that we see things existing, and it is not so. Therefore, we are not sure of the existence of God; for it rests upon our mendacious faculties.

Des Cartes, therefore, never got beyond his *cogito, ergo sum*. This is both the beginning and the end of his philosophy. The only important truth which he signalized is, *That the ultimate organ of science consists in an appeal to the facts of consciousness.* But this truth he arbitrarily limits to self-consciousness, and as arbitrarily applies it to the outward world, through the false assumption of an innate idea of God; thus creating or assuming a chasm where none exists, and then bridging it over with a figment of his imagination. His denial of the contemporaneousness of the knowledge of one's self and of the outward world, at once ignored the possibility of any knowledge at all of external nature, and put the mind on that track of preposterous speculation of endeavouring to bridge the imaginary chasm between the subjective and the objective, which could only, from such a starting-point, end in the identification of the last with the first; and thus commute the subjective with the objective, to a degree of extravagance that would make Bacon smile at the smallness of the same error in the ancient philosophy, which his whole method was designed to counteract. In the philosophy of Des Cartes, in fact, begun that exaltation of human reason, which, in the philosophy of Schelling and Hegel, ended in the dethronement of God, and the inauguration of man to the sceptre of omniscience.

The extraordinary influence which the philosophy of Des Cartes has exerted on modern speculation, is, therefore, in our judgment, to be attributed rather to its ministering to a cardinal weakness of the human mind, *the tendency to a priori speculation*, than to any force of truth in its doctrines or of forecast in its regulative principle of method. This method is an arbitrary formula, as inapplicable in the hunting-ground of investigation as the stereotyped forms of the schoolmen. The provisional doubt, the *assumed* conviction that truth is possible, and the *cogito, ergo sum*, as a direction to the inquirer, are but a beggarly account of empty boxes. It must lead to *a priori* speculation, disjoined from the *a posteriori* elements of thought, to an unmitigated Idealism or Rationalism. Nothing can show more clearly the bias of Des Cartes towards a demonstrative or rationalistic philosophy, than the fact that, in his attempt to express the simultaneity and identity of *the knowing that we think, and the knowing that we exist, that they are but one indivisible deliverance of consciousness*, he enunciates it in a form of expression which indicates a relation of subordination and sequence; *cogito, ergo sum*. The external expression is certainly an enthymeme with a suppressed major, whatever the internal thought of the thinker was. The expression is certainly not a simple affirmation of the identity of thought and being in the sphere of consciousness, but indicates both the priority of self in consciousness, and that the notion of self and the notion of being are found apart and are conjoined through the higher principle—*what thinks, is*. This bias at the starting-point is impressed on the whole Cartesian philosophy.

In estimating the value of the Cartesian philosophy, two things have been confounded, which, if not distinguished, must involve us in the most perplexing confusions. By no one have these two things been more signally confounded than by Cousin, the learned and brilliant editor of the works of Des Cartes. Speaking of two little tracts by Des Cartes, he says: "We see in these more unequivocally the main object of Des Cartes, and the spirit of the revolution which has created modern philosophy, and placed in the understanding itself the principle of all certainty, the point of departure for all legitimate inquiry." The great error in this passage is the making "the principle of all certainty *the point of departure* for all legitimate inquiry." This is the germinal vice of the Cartesian philosophy. In the regressive analysis, by which we pass backward to the basis of certainty, we arrive at consciousness as the ultimate arbiter, the last oracle. But, to make this the *point of departure*, as Des Cartes did, for inquiry into philosophy, is erroneous, and was the great blunder in the Cartesian method. From facts of consioussness, "seeds of truth in the mind," as he called them, Des Cartes even essayed to project the system of the physical universe, and thereby make the physical sciences mere educts of the understanding. He restored the ancient method of reasoning *a priori*, from causes to effects. Facts of observation must be the starting-point in all philosophy, whether mental or physical. Des Cartes reversed the scholastic proposition, and made it read, *Nihil est in sensu, quod non fuit prius in intellectu.*

The philosophy of Des Cartes had produced upon the thinking of the succeeding age an impression adverse to the whole Baconian method. It had given an extreme subjective turn to thought. This subjective character would be the point of attack by any one taking the Baconian view of philosophizing. Therefore it was that Locke, in the very beginning of his Essay on the Human Understanding, enters upon the question of the origin of our ideas or knowledge. This question involves the problem of the objectivity and subjectivity of knowledge. We think, therefore, that the criticism of Cousin and others, that Locke's method is entirely wrong, because of his entering upon this question before determining what are the actual products of thought in the maturely developed consciousness, is entirely futile. The origin of our knowledge was the problem lying at the threshold of the issue between the objective method of Bacon and the subjective method of Des Cartes. If all science could be excogitated, *a priori*, out of human reason, with some little resort to external observation, as Des Cartes maintained, then the Baconian method, which placed the possibility of science exclusively in the observation of the invariable coexistence, and the invariable antecedence and sequence of the phenomena of nature, was a grovelling puerility. How, therefore, could this antagonism between the subjective and the objective methods be determined, but by considering how far thought is objective, and how far subjective? It is in fact a discussion of method in its ultimate analysis. The discussion of the origin of knowledge was demanded by the polemical conditions of thought at that day. Progress was impossible until the problem was laid open. And however weak Locke's discussion of the doctrine of innate ideas may be, when viewed under the higher light of the present times, it did great good in its day. It gave insight into the problem of subjectivity, in a form that would be appreciated by the largest number of minds, and make them ignore the subjective method. It matters not, therefore, so far as the fortunes of philosophy are concerned, whether Des Cartes or any other philosopher ever held the doctrine of innate ideas in the form in which Locke exhibits it. He chose to exhibit the error of subjectivity in such a form as that in which—according to his judgment, and in this we believe he was right—it presented itself to most thinkers of those times. Indeed, after the most careful consideration of the subject in all its bearings, we cannot but believe that Des Cartes *assumed,* at least in his philosophy, a doctrine of innate ideas almost precisely such as Locke presents it. It is true, that when Gassendi charged upon him the doctrine, much as Locke afterwards exhibited it, he swallowed half that he had written, and said he only meant by innate ideas, innate faculties. This, however, avails, we confess, nothing with us; for, in those parts of his method, where he maintains that from a few *a priori* principles *assumed as facts of consciousness,* he could evolve by logical deduction what was the mode in which suns, planets, water, light, minerals, plants, animals—the last, however, he admits, require ample experiments—must have been, or at least *may* have been successively constituted, he certainly assumes a psychological basis of thought substantially the same with Locke's doctrine of innate ideas. "The order (says Des Cartes) I pursued, was this: First, I endeavoured to discover, in general, the principles or first causes of everything which is or can be in the world, *without considering anything for this purpose, except God alone, who has created it, nor deducing these principles from aught else than from certain seeds of truth which exist naturally in our souls.* After that, I examined what would be the first and most ordinary effects which might be deduced from these causes; and it seems to me that I could hence discover heavens, stars, and earth, and even upon that earth, water, air, fire, minerals, and some other things which are the most easy to be known." This is but the general doctrine of method expounded in the writings of Des Cartes. The "seeds of truth," existing naturally in the soul, are spoken of by Leibnitz and by Cudworth, both of whom are Idealists, the first much the same as Des Cartes, the latter a little more Platonic: but both maintaining, or at least assuming, a doctrine in its logical import much like the doctrine of innate ideas presented by Locke, which, however, be it remembered, Locke ascribes to no one in particular.

We, therefore, dissent from those who think Locke's discussion of innate ideas of little importance in the progress of philosophy; but, with the qualifications which we have stated, we are ready to admit that

Locke's philosophy is weak on its negative side—its hostile discussion of the *a priori* element of human thought. But on its positive side, its account of the origin of our ideas or knowledge, it is all that could have been expected in his time.

From the fact, that Locke opposed with so much earnestness the doctrine of innate ideas, he has been represented, by many, as a pure Sensationalist, one who believes that all our knowledge is derived from or through the senses. A more erroneous interpretation of an author was never recorded in the pages of criticism. The blunder is a marvel of misapprehension. However far Locke's account of the origin of our ideas may fall short of the whole truth, as we readily admit it does, it certainly, in the most explicit manner, maintains that our ideas are derived from two sources, sensation or sensitive perception, and reflection or self-consciousness. "External objects (says Locke) furnish the mind with ideas of sensible qualities; and the mind furnishes the understanding with the ideas of its own operations. The understanding seems to me not to have the least glimmering of any ideas which it doth not receive from one of these two sources." How criticism has brought itself to interpret this and numberless other passages, in which Locke distinctly and carefully affirms that there are two different sources of our ideas, sensation and reflection, so as to make Locke resolve them into one, is strange enough, and but evinces the perversity of human judgment. And Cousin, with all the light to the contrary, which Dugald Stewart, in his Preliminary Dissertation, had shed upon the question, pronounces Locke a Sensationalist. Enslaved by the spirit of a system which required him to find in Locke the root of the Sensationalism of the eighteenth century, he says: "Locke is the father of the whole Sensualistic school of the eighteenth century. He is incontestably, in time as well as genius, the first metaphysician of this school." The vile Sensualism or Sensationalism of Condillac and Cabanis is thus made a justifiable extension of Locke's philosophy — fruit springing legitimately from the germ which Locke planted in the fields of thought. And prone, with a predisposition increased by the heat of progress, to exaggerate every indication of Sensationalism in the writings of Locke, he maintains that Locke makes an interval between the time of acquiring the ideas of sensation and those of reflection; and thus opens the way for the theory of "transformed sensations"— of sensation as the sole principle of all the operations of the soul. This is a shallow criticism. The purpose of Locke was to rescue philosophy from subjectivity, and turn observation upon the objective. Whether by *innate ideas* Des Cartes meant something coeval in its existence with the mind to which it belongs, and illuminating the understanding before the external senses begin to operate, or not, as Locke supposed, certainly the great tendency of his philosophy was to commute the subjective with the objective —to lead to a high *a priori* philosophy and science— to turn back the Baconian movement by reversing its method. The task, therefore, of Locke's philosophy was to restore the Baconian method by developing its psychological basis. Therefore, repudiating all knowledges prior to experience beginning in the senses, Locke says: "If it be demanded when a man begins to have any ideas, I think the true answer is, when he first has any sensation. I conceive that ideas in the understanding are coeval with sensation." Locke then enounces two sources of ideas, in the passage which we have already quoted; and, in accordance with the principle that sensation is prior to all ideas in the undestanding, he treats of the ideas of sensation first, and of reflection second; being induced to do this by the great purpose of his philosophy—to throw observation upon external nature. But that Locke meant to assert that there is an interval of time between our knowledge of matter and of mind, cannot be maintained; and least of all, that *the knowledge of matter has the priority.* It really mortifies us that these stale criticisms, which make Locke a mere Sensationalist, should be written anew in the history of philosophy by a countryman of Locke's at this late day.* Mr. Morrell has, as it were, permitted Cousin to hold his hand while he writes the history of philosophy. He has, therefore, divided all philosophers into two classes, Sensationalists and Idealists. This division is based upon the supposition, that Eclecticism is the true account of the develpment of philosophy. This view of the development of philosophy, taught him by Cousin, led him to follow that philosopher in his strictures upon Locke, and class him amongst Sensationalists. Eclecticism assumes that no one man, from the very necessary order of philosophical development, can lay open the foundations of philosophy broad enough to bear the superstructure — can lay open sufficiently sensation and self-consciousness as sources of knowledge. It postulates, that every philosopher and his age has developed either the one or the other of these sources of knowledge, but never both. And that, in the order of things, a great mind, endowed with a universal genius

* M. Cousin in 1853 published an edition of his Lectures on The True, Beautiful, and Good, "severely corrected," intended as a summary of his philosophy, and his "last word — his final lecture." In this admirable resumé, he has so modified his doctrines, that we beg the reader to read this final work by Cousin, that it may be seen amongst other things that he has retreated a good deal from the opinion of Locke which we have attributed to him, and which we should have modified, had we read this work of M. Cousin before we wrote this book, as well as noticed particularly what he has said about his philosophy being called *eclecticism*.

of criticism, and possessed of all learning in philosophy, must discover a higher method than had thus far been pursued—the method of Eclecticism, a method assumed to be as far above induction and reflective analysis, as the eclectic philosopher is above those one-idea philosophers who, given up to either Sensationalism or Idealism, are his necessary forerunners in the development of philosophy. But this boasted Eclecticism, when searched to the bottom, is discovered to be a mere scheme of compilation, a universal plagiarism.

As we can know things only in so far as we have a faculty of knowing in general, it is necessary, in order to a true theory of knowledge, that we determine the scope of this faculty. This Locke endeavoured to do. He maintained that all our knowledge is obtained through observation. He further maintained that the faculties of observation are two: 1. Sense, or external perception; 2. Self-consciousness, or internal perception. The fundamental problem, therefore, of Locke's philosophy, was to determine the conditions of our faculties of knowing. But Locke did not see this problem very definitely, if at all.

All knowledge is divisible into two great branches: 1. *The objects of knowledge;* 2. *The mode of knowing.* The objects of knowledge Locke properly divided into two great classes, external and internal, corresponding to his two faculties of *sense* and *reflection* or self-consciousness. The mode of knowing is also divisible into two parts: 1. *The possibility of knowing from the nature of thought;* 2. *The possibility of knowing from the nature of existence.* This last discrimination Locke had no notion of. The problem of the conditions of knowledge, therefore, never presented itself distinctly to Locke. It is true, that occasionally he is constrained by the exigencies of thought to utter truths which properly fall under the problem of the conditions of thought. He says, for instance: "He would be thought void of *common sense* who, asked on the one hand or on the other, were to give a reason why it is impossible for the same thing to be and not to be." Here is a distinct recognition of the principle of contradiction, which, of course, has its origin and guarantee in the intellect or common sense. Locke, too, believed in necessary and universal truths, as distinguished from contingent; which, of course, can only find their guarantee in the intellect, being in no way derivable from or through sensitive cognition. And in this criterion of certainty he was extremely subjective, maintaining that the subjective in knowledge is much more certain than the objective; thereby erroneously ignoring the simultaneity of the subjective and objective in the fundamental antithesis of consciousness, and the consequent equal certainty of each. "Our existence (says Locke) is known to us by a certainty yet higher than our senses can give us of the existence of things, and that is internal perception, or self-consciousness, or intuition, from whence may be drawn, by a train of ideas, the surest and most incontestable proof of the existence of God." This, surely, is not the doctrine of a mere Sensationalist. If Locke had been called by the polemical necessities of his times to consider the *conditions of thought* as a special problem, he would doubtless have evolved other principles similar to those we have just mentioned; and, while he would have denied that they are innate, as articulate propositions, he would have admitted that they are silent in laws necessitating thought to its judgments. For it should be observed that Locke's essay was not the mere theory of a recluse student, but had a polemical birth in the midst of an age in which the discussion of great fundamental doctrines were stirring, in an extraordinary degree, the practical activities of life. Locke was a mighty champion in the universal strife; and his essay was written to counteract the subjective tendency of the Cartesian philosophy. Hence the great stress laid on sensation as a source of knowledge or ideas, to the comparative neglect of the other source, termed by him reflection. But it is only a *comparative* neglect; for, in the first place, he purges, as we have seen, the source of reflection from the doctrine of innate ideas, which, in a logical point of view, are substantially the idols of Bacon. Then, after carefully affirming the existence of two sources of ideas, he proceeds, in accordance with the demands of philosophy in that age, to develop the source of sensation. Locke's philosophy is, therefore, not a one-sided philosophy. Like Bacon, Locke was a labourer in the great field of practical activity. Not only was he a physician skilled in the practice, and well read in the theory of medicine, but he was a powerful writer on government and legislation, and not only these, but a polemic, strong in theological discussion. To estimate, therefore, the mental theory of Locke's essay, it is necessary to view it through the medium of the times, and of the part he took in the strifes of thought. But what is chiefly to be praised in Locke's writings, is the love of truth which everywhere prevails. "Whatever I write (says he), as soon as I shall discover it not to be *truth*, my hand shall be forwardest to throw it into the fire."

Locke had enounced the doctrine that all our knowledge is founded on experience, meaning by experience the whole sphere of conscious mental activity, thereby embracing in it reflection as well as sensation. Hume, seizing upon this doctrine, and narrowing experience to sensation, resolved all our universal necessary judgments into mere factitious habits of mind, and subverted the foundations of theoretical truth, and laid the basis of a scheme of absolute skepticism. For, if our fundamental primary judgments are not necessary, but are mere habits of mind formed from the observation of the contingent, coexistent, and antecedent, and consequent, phenomena of external nature, then is human opinion but waves of thought moved by the accidents of the shifting winds of ever-changing phenomena; and what seems true this moment may seem false the next. This chaos of thought was brought into order and certainty by Reid. He it was who evolved out of the contents of human consciousness those fundamental, necessary, primary beliefs, which constitute both the basis and the criterion of human knowledge. In Locke's time, the vice of philosophy was too great subjectivity. In Reid's time, it was a total abnegation of all certain knowledge, but especially of those fundamental judgments which alone fix certainty in thought—a vice which sprung out of the extravagant objectivity to which Locke's philosophy had been carried by Hume, confining all thought to the elements furnished by sensation. If Hobbes and Gassendi had obtained in Britain as great ascendency in Locke's time as Hume did in Reid's, Locke would perhaps have dwelt as much more on reflection as he did on sensation, and the philosophy of Reid would have been anticipated. But, in the conditions of the development of human thought, it was perhaps necessary that the development by Locke should take place, so that its apparent one-sidedness should appear in Hume, and thus a necessity be produced for a re-examination of human thought to its ultimate basis in the primary facts of consciousness. Reid, therefore, in fact, took up philosophy where Locke left it, and continued the Baconian movement, with a fuller development of the subjective than there was in Locke, but still guided by the fundamental doctrine of Bacon, that truth consists in the correspondence or agreement between thought and its object; and that, in order to secure the truth, observation of phenomena is the indispensable condition. The movement was still towards a fuller outward observation of external nature. And the Baconian method received a fuller theoretical development in the psychological doctrine of Reid, that we perceive external objects themselves, as consciousness testifies, and not merely representations of them, as all previous philosophers had taught. And by his doctrine of the simultaneity and consequent equal certainty of the knowledge of the objective and the subjective, Reid overthrew the doctrine of Des Cartes, that our knowledge of external things must be referred by a secondary act of thought to consciousness for verification. And in this doctrine of Reid, for the first time in philosophy, the subjective and the objective obtained their equilibrium. In his philosophy neither preponderates over the other. While, therefore, in the philosophy of Reid, the subjective is prevented from being commuted with the objective, the certainty of the objective is equalized with the subjective.

But it came to pass, that the doctrines of Reid were misrepresented and perverted by Brown, and the Sensationalism of Destutt Tracy of France, and kindred doctrines of Hume, diluted with rhetoric, were proclaimed by him in their stead. Brown made consciousness convertible with feeling; and the thought, that *the whole is greater than its part,* is considered by him as a feeling. Thus the most extravagant Sensationalism again prevailed in Britain. And though the proud boast of Bacon—that, so potent was his induction as a method of investigation, that it would put common minds on a level with the most powerful—had not been realized, yet it brought into the fields of physical science the merest empirics in company with true sciencists. Thus the downward tendency of physical inquiry needed to be counteracted by a discipline of higher studies. Human reason needed to be rescued from the dirt of a gross Sensationalism.

While this downward tendency of the objective method of Bacon had been realized in Britain, the subjective method of Des Cartes had been realizing its results on the continent of Europe. In the philosophy of Spinosa, it tended to Pantheism. In that of Leibnitz, from its opposite pole, it made man a mere machine, and the physical world his counterpart, moving in harmony, not by interdependent cog-wheels, but by an unseen spiritual agency; which doctrine, when sifted to the kernel, is also of Pantheistic tendency. But under the influence of the Cartesian method, enlarged in its scope to suit the necessities of its condition, human reason, at last, in the philosophy of Schelling and Hegel, consummated the grand apotheosis of error, by throwing aside the many idols of the ancient philosophy pointed out by Bacon, and substituting for them one supreme idol, impiously called the Absolute or Infinite.

But the greatest degradation of philosophy remains to be told. The prejudice against the Aristotelian logic, which begun in Bacon, was augmented by Locke; so that logic was almost ignored in Britain. The marvels accomplished in physics, by co-operation, through the method of induction, gave importance to men whose moderate abilities would ever exclude them from the higher study of our intellectual nature; while the patient attention to details, which physical inquiries demand, caused an almost exclusive cultivation of the powers of observation, to the neglect of the higher faculties of the mind. Logic, therefore, as well as metaphysics, sunk to the lowest level, in the almost exclusive cultivation of physics.

In this state of philosophy, Archbishop Whately revived logic, in a work not displaying any great ability, but, at all events, attracting the attention of thinkers. The work did not, however, place logic on that elevation which the indications of its history in the mediæval and the succeeding ages would have pointed out to any one well read in its literature. Nevertheless, it was an omen of the beginning of the cultivation of the higher faculties of the mind in an age of intellectual decadence. But, as low as the level of Whately's logic was, it was too high for the empiric spirit of a Sensational philosophy. Mr. John S. Mill, in his Logic, Ratiocinative and Inductive, dragged down logic into the very mire of empiricism. Taking Brown, who, we have seen, makes consciousness convertible with feeling, as his guide in the philosophy of the mind, he constructed a system of logic in which the higher faculties of the mind are ignored. While Whately, with some show of reason, resolved induction into deduction or syllogism proper, Mill most preposterously resolved all deduction into induction; and thereby consummated the degradation of logic. Mr. Mill repudiates entirely all necessary truths; consequently ignores the formal laws of thought, of which pure logic is the science, and reduces all thought to the uncertainty of the empirical conditions of observation. He ignores all distinction between the apodictic and the hypothetical exercise of the understanding. He seems never to consider, that the determinations of the understanding are often effected solely by the relation in which intelligence stands to itself in thought. He maintains that deduction is but an extension of induction, and from the beginning to the end of his exposition confounds *inference* with *deduction.* The intrusion of matter between the premises and the conclusion of a syllogism, which is the cardinal error to be guarded against in logic, is the very thing which Mr. Mill strives to effect as the great end and consummation of correct reasoning. The syllogism is founded upon matter which it passively receives. It does not even develop potential knowledge into actual, but merely evolves implicit knowledge into explicit. The conclusion is already known before the syllogism is formed. Ratiocination is determined by the relations into which intelligence puts itself to itself in regard to some object-matter. Such being the nature of ratiocination, its very form in the syllogism excludes everything intrusive between the premises and the conclusion. In a word, Mr. Mill does not discriminate pure logic, wherein the mental determinations are effected by the formal laws of thought, from concrete or modified logic, wherein the mental determinations are effected under the laws of thought, modified by the empirical circumstances under which we exert our faculties. But even in concrete or modified logic, thought is not considered as applied to any particular matter, but the necessary are considered in conjunction with the contingent conditions under which thought is actually exerted. Mr. Mill does not discriminate pure from applied logic, formal from material illation, but confounds them.

It may be said, in answer to these strictures, that Mr. Mill defines in the beginning of his treatise what scope he intends to give it, and that the objection we make is one merely of the meaning of words. This mode of answering our objection, while it has the air of looking at the subject from a more comprehensive point of view, is a sheer evasion. Mr. Mill has not the right to confuse the boundaries of a science. Logic is found by reflective analysis as well as by the indications of its history to be confined to the formal laws of thought as its adequate object-matter; else all the material sciences must be intruded into it. Mr. Mill, therefore, by taking into logic so much foreign matter, is like a geographer who should take into the map of America the continent of Europe. But Mr. Mill's is not merely an error of boundary: it is a blunder in all the fundamental doctrines of logic, leading him to repeat, with emphasis, the stale misapprehension, that Bacon's method is one-sided, excluding deduction altogether as a process of investigation. Playfair, in his celebrated Dissertation on the Progress of the Mathematical and Physical Sciences, pronounced the same judgment, and disparaged Bacon's method as Mr. Mill does, by saying that it ignored the process which in the advanced stage of the sciences becomes the most important and effective. Whereas, what Mr. Mill and his forerunners in the error call deduction, is not deduction, a demonstrative process, at all, but is what

Bacon means by the descending scale of induction, being in fact a hypothetical and not an apodictic process, and is sometimes, as we have already shown, called the synthetical process of induction. The blunder of Mr. Mill is thus a double one; first, in supposing the process to be deduction when it is not; secondly, in supposing that Bacon excluded it from his method. The truth is, Bacon strode with such colossal steps along the paths of philosophy, that but few have been able to step in his exact footprints, and of these few Mr. Mill is not one, as his numerous misapprehensions of Bacon's method show.

But the most mischievous error which derationalizes Mr. Mill's logic, is the notion, that "Deduction is the great scientific work of the present and future ages;" and that "a revolution is peaceably and progressively effecting itself in philosophy, the reverse of that to which Bacon has attached his name." This doctrine, assuming as it does, that the highest generalities have been reached, evinces a narrowness of comprehension, which of itself would put Mr. Mill below any very high elevation as a thinker; but when it is also a broad contradiction of the fundamental doctrine of his system of logic, which resolves deduction into induction, Mr. Mill stands revealed as a thinker who does not understand himself, but crosses his own path in his exposition of doctrines; and the best refutation is to leave him in the entanglement of his own contradictions.

Induction has been also signally corrupted by Dr. Whewell, in his Philosophy of the Inductive Sciences. The inductive process, according to Dr. Whewell, consists in selecting conceptions which exist in the mind anterior to all experience, and by these binding together the objects of observation, in conformity with certain relations subsisting between the percepts derived from the objects, and the conceptions or ideas of colligation. The operation proceeds by trying, first, one conception, or idea of colligation, and then another, until the right one is found. Now, if the process of induction were that of binding phenomena together by certain innate ideas or conceptions, as Whewell contends, it would be just as easy to find the proper idea of colligation on seeing a few phenomena, as on seeing many. Because it seems sufficiently manifest, that a number of instances outside of the mind could in no way enable us any more readily to find the idea of colligation amid the multitude of such, which, *ex hypothesi*, exist in the mind, to bind together the given instances, than the given instances themselves would. For, in the given instances themselves, the fitness of the idea of colligation must appear; and yet, the inductive inference or idea of colligation is only suggested by many instances. In this truth alone, is found a sufficient refutation of Whewell's theory of the idea of colligation.

The tendency of this doctrine of Dr. Whewell's, is

to set up in the mind a physical standard of things, and thus commute the subjective with the objective. The doctrine springs out of a misunderstanding of the manner in which the mind comes by concepts, or, as Dr. Whewell improperly calls them, conceptions. The mind cannot embrace many objects at once; it must single out one, and, when this is done, all others are excluded. The product of the mind, when attention is thus given to one object only, is a percept. But the mind strives to comprehend many objects also. It, therefore, by comparing objects, discovers similarities between them, and it dwells upon the characters which constitute their similarity to the exclusion of the characters which constitute their dissimilarity, and identifies the similarities, and expresses the identification by a general term. The product of the mind, in such identification of similarities, is a concept. Now, Dr. Whewell's ideas of colligation are only these concepts empirically formed from observation; and the colligation of which he speaks is done in the very act of conception—is, in fact, the concept itself. The concept thus formed may then be used in binding together similar objects or phenomena. His doctrine of ideas of colligation is, therefore, a gross absurdity, which vitiates his whole philosophy, and, together with other similar errors, degrades him to a low level as an expounder of logical philosophy. In truth, Dr. Whewell is as crude and confused a thinker as ever aspired with such laborious ambition to be a philosopher.

The philosophy of the Absolute and Infinite, has, too, its own pretended method, called the ontological method. In this philosophy, logic, in any proper sense, is done away with. Assuming a faculty of intellectual intuition, by which the absolute and the infinite are immediately perceived, it repudiates altogether as beneath the high purposes of philosophy, the grovelling method of induction. Its method of investigation, if it can be called so, is not a process of inference founded upon evidence, but is an immediate intuition, where reasoning becomes only tracing, intellectually, the order of creation as it proceeded by evolution from its primordial element of absolute being. This method claims to evolve all human knowledge, and all that is knowable, out of one fundamental entity, in which subject and object, God and man, Creator and creature, are identified. Its process of evolution is identical with the process of creation. As creation is the process of Almighty thought, resulting in all that exists, so human thought, in the ontological method, is the similar process of a finite mind, resulting in the knowledge of all that exists—the same process of the finite mind being subordinated to result only in knowledge, while that of the infinite results in creation.*

* The Hegelians say, the end of philosophy is to rethink the great thought of creation.

Such is as articulate a statement as we are able to give of the method of a philosophy which commutes the nescience of man with the omniscience of God; and which, when sifted to the bottom, is found to be an antithesis of the broadest contradictions.

We have now exhibited the state of philosophy that has resulted from both the Baconian and Cartesian movements. The Scotch philosopher, Sir William Hamilton, had begun a reclamation of philosophy. We will consider his labours in the second part of this tract. We designate the time in which he flourished, and which is still in progress, as a reactionary epoch. Our criticisms will, therefore, be both retrospective and prospective. Topics already passed in review will be considered, though in new relations.

# PROGRESS OF PHILOSOPHY.

## Part Second.

### REACTIONARY EPOCH.

THOUGH of Lord Bacon it was said, by his friend, Dr. Harvey, the discoverer of the circulation of the blood, "he writes philosophy like a Lord Chancellor," it must be admitted, Sir William Hamilton writes it like a philosopher. For he both thinks and writes, more like a pure intelligence, than any man in the history of speculation. In the first place, his diction is the most concise, the most accurate, the most direct, the most compact, and the most vigorous ever used by any writer on philosophy. Familiar with all systems of philosophy ever proposed, and their criticisms, expository, supplementary and adverse, and a master of the languages in which both the philosophies and the criticisms have been written; he has discovered how much of their errors can be ascribed to the deficiencies of language, both as an instrument and as a vehicle of philosophical thought; and he has, accordingly, formed a language for himself, adequate to the exigencies of the highest thinking, in the new career of philosophy which he has inaugurated. And his learning, in every department of knowledge supplementary of philosophy, or auxiliary to it, is so abundant, that there seems to be not even a random thought of any value, which has been dropped along any, even obscure, path of mental activity, in any age or country, that his diligence has not recovered, his sagacity appreciated, and his judgment husbanded in the stores of his knowledge. And, in discussing any question of philosophy, his ample learning enables him to classify all the different theories which have, at successive periods, been invented to explain it; and generally, indeed we may say always, he discovers, by the light reciprocally shed from the theories, ideas involved in them which their respective advocates had not discriminated; thereby giving greater accuracy to the theories than they had before. By this mode of discussion, we have the history of doctrines concentrated into a focus of elucidation. And the uses of words, and the mutations in their meaning, in different languages, are articulately set forth; thereby enhancing the accuracy and certainty of our footsteps on the slippery paths of speculation. And his own genius for original research is such, that no subtlety of our intelligent nature, however evasive, no relation however indirect or remote, no manifestation however ambiguous or obscure, can escape or elude his critical diagnosis. Add to all this; his moral constitution, both by nature and by education, is harmonious with his intellectual, imparting to his faculties the energy of a well-directed will, and the wisdom of a pure love of truth. Therefore it is, that in the writings of Sir William Hamilton there is nothing of that vacillation in doctrine which results from unbalanced faculties. He has built upon the same foundation from the beginning. Another notable characteristic is his extraordinary individuality. He seems, in no degree, under the influence of what is called the doctrine of the historical development of human intelligence. He confronts the whole history of doctrines, and with a cold critical eye surveys them as the products of individual minds, and not as the evolutions of a total humanity. Of eclecticism, there is in his creed not the smallest taint. Truth seems to him the same everywhere, unmodified by times. Such is the marvellous man, of whose philosophy we propose to give some account.

The history of philosophy seems, to the superficial observer, but the recurrence of successive cycles of the same problems, the same discussions, and the same opinions. He sees, in modern philosophy, only the repetition of the dreams of the earliest Greek speculators. Philosophy is to him but labour upon an insoluble problem. To the competent critic, however, it presents a far different view. He sees, in each cycle, new aspects of the problems, new relations in the discussions, and new modes in the opinions—all indicating an advancement, however unequal and halting at times, towards the truth. Here then is, at once, evinced the supreme importance of an enlightened philosophical criticism. It is the preparative and precursor of further progress. The different doctrines which, in successive ages, have been elicited, are so many experiments, furnishing, to the enlightened critic, indications more or less obvious of the true solutions of the problems of philosophy.

Sir William Hamilton is the prince of critics in philosophy. In him philosophical criticism has compassed its widest scope, and reached its highest attainments. He is the critic of all ages, equally at home in all. He has sifted all of ancient, all of mediæval, and all of modern thought, with the most delicate sieve ever used by any critic; and while he has winnowed away the chaff, he has lost not a grain of truth. The barriers of different languages have not excluded him from a single field: he unlocked the gates of one as easily as another, and entered where he listed. With principles of criticism as broad as nature, with learning as extensive as the whole of what has been written on philosophy, with a knowledge of words, and of the things which they denote or are intended to denote, marvellously accurate and coextensive with the whole literature of speculation, with a logic both in its pure theory and modified applications, adequate to every need of intelligence, whether in detecting the fallacies or expounding the truths of doctrine, and with a genius exactly suited to use, with the greatest effect, these manifold accomplishments, he stands pre-eminent amongst the critics of philosophy. As we have seen how he unravels the network of entangled discussions, discriminating the confusions by purifying the doctrines through a more adequate conception and expression of them, often correcting the text of the Greek writer, which for centuries had baffled the grammarians, by the light of the doctrine of the author, and in the sequel making the truth educed the starting-point for new development of doctrine, we have admired the matchless abilities of the critic, until we should have been exhausted in being dragged along the labyrinths of his mighty ratiocination, had we not been refreshed at every turn by the new light of truth disclosed by the master who was conducting the marvellous enterprise of thought. Bentley did not do more to enlarge the scope, and enrich the learning of British literary criticism, when, by his dissertations on the Epistles of Phalaris, he raised it from the platitudes of the grammarian and the rhetorician to the compass, the life, the interest, and the dignity of philological and historical disquisition, than Sir William Hamilton has done to give profundity, subtlety, comprehensiveness, and erudition to British philosophical criticism, by his contributions to the *Edinburgh Review*. These articles mark an era, not only in British but in European criticism in every department of philosophy—metaphysics, psychology, and logic. They were translated into the languages of the continent, and their stupendous learning, matchless subtlety, and ruthless ratiocination, received everywhere unbounded admiration. The very first article, the one on the doctrine of the infinito-absolute of Cousin, utterly subverted the fundamentals of the proud speculations of Germany, and fully exposed the absurdity of the attempt of Cousin to conciliate them with the humble Scottish philosophy of common sense. The continental philosophers saw that a critic had arisen, who, by the might and the majesty of his intellect, and the vastness of his erudition, gave dignity to the humble doctrine which he advocated, and they had all along despised. They began to feel,

> "A chiel's amang us takin' notes,
> And faith, he'll prent it."

But Sir William Hamilton, the critic, is only the precursor of Sir William Hamilton the philosopher. His criticism is but the preparative of his philosophy. They, however, move on together. The state of the philosophy of the world made this necessary. The calling of Socrates was not more determined by the condition of thought in his time, than the labours of Sir

William Hamilton are by the philosophical needs of this age. His erudition and critical skill are as much needed as his matchless genius for original speculation. Either, without the other, would have been comparatively barren of results. And his preference, like Aristotle, for logic rather than the other branches of philosophy, is the very affection that is desiderated in the great thinker of this age. It seems to be supposed by some, who even pretend to have studied the philosophy of Sir William Hamilton, that he has merely rehabilitated the doctrines of Reid and Stewart. It might, with much more show of truth be said, that Newton only reproduced the discoveries of Copernicus and Kepler. For the philosophy of Sir William Hamilton is a greater stride beyond that of his Scottish predecessors, than the discoveries and deductions of Newton are beyond those of Copernicus and Kepler. Let us then, as far as his published writings and our limits will permit, show what Sir William has done directly to advance philosophy.

With Bacon began a movement in modern philosophy, which parallels that begun by Aristotle in ancient.* Aristotle inaugurated the deductive process;

* When we say that Bacon and Aristotle began these respective movements, we do not mean literally, that the movements originated with them, but only that, like Luther's in the Reformation, their labours were so signal and paramount, in these movements, as to be associated pre-eminently with them.

Bacon inaugurated the inductive. These are the distinctive features of those systems of philosophy which they advocated; and they are in accordance with the spirit of philosophizing in the respective periods to which they belonged. Ancient philosophy was more a deduction from principles; modern philosophy is more an inquiry into principles themselves. Aristotle and Bacon both make logic the paramount branch of philosophy; and the forms of the understanding the limits of the knowable. Sir William Hamilton's philosophy is a preparative and an initial towards the conciliation of the systems of Aristotle and Bacon. Logic, with him as with them, is the paramount branch of philosophy; and his labours all tend to reconcile induction with deduction, and unify in one method these two great processes of thought. His philosophy is, in fact, a climateric reclamation, vindication, and development of the one perennial philosophy of common sense, which, like the one true faith, is preserved amidst all schismatic aberrations, and vindicated as the only true philosophy.

---

No great change ever originates with the person who becomes the most conspicuous in it, in the great spectacle of history. It always has antecedents, produced by the agency of inferior persons. We, therefore, beg, that everywhere, in this tract, the principle of this note may qualify our general remarks, even in regard to the claims of originality, which we prefer for Sir William Hamilton, unless our remarks preclude qualification.

It is in the essential unity of human reason returning again and again, from temporary aberrations in different ages, into the same discernments and convictions, that we have the means of verifying the true catholic philosophy. Though there may be nothing in the mutual relations of men, at any given time, nor in the mutual relations of successive generations, that necessarily determines an uninterrupted advance towards truth, yet, notwithstanding the occasional wide-spread and long protracted prevalence of error, the reason of man has hitherto vindicated itself in the long run, and proved that, though the newest phase of thought may not, at all times, be the truest, yet the truest will prevail at last, and come out at the goal of human destiny, triumphant over all errors. This is the drift of the history of human opinion as interpreted by enlightened criticism. Sometimes skepticism, recognizing no criterion of truth; sometimes idealism, knowing nothing but images in ceaseless change; sometimes pantheism, dissolving all individuality, both material and spiritual, in the tides of universal being; sometimes materialism, believing nothing beyond material nature, and that man is only a more perfect species of mammalia, and human affairs but the highest branch of natural history; and other forms of error, each with its peculiar momenta and criteria of knowledge, have in reiterated succession, in different ages of the world, prevailed as systems of philosophy; yet the reason of man has, nevertheless, under the guidance of some master mind, returned to the one perennial philosophy of common sense, and reposed in the natural conviction of mankind, that an external world exists as the senses testify, and that there is in man an element which lifts him above the kingdom of nature, and allies him in responsible personal individuality with a divine, eternal, and personal God.

The great office of the critic of philosophy, at this day, is to trace the footsteps of this perennial philosophy through the history of human opinion in all its manifold mutations, perversions, and aberrations; and to note its features, observe the paths it walks in, and its method and criteria of truth. This Sir William Hamilton has done. He has shown that the doctrine of common sense, as the basis of all philosophy, has prevailed for more than two thousand years. He has adduced one hundred and six witnesses, Greek, Roman, Arabian, Italian, Spanish, French, British, German, and Belgian, to its truth. Amongst the many Greek witnesses, Aristotle is found; amongst the Roman, Cicero; amongst the Italians, Aquinas; amongst the French, all the great philosophers from Des Cartes to Cousin, both inclusive; amongst the Germans, Leibnitz, Kant, Jacobi, and even Fichte, with a host of others; thus showing, that what is sometimes thought, even by those from whom we might expect better things, to be the superficial foundation of British philosophy, is in truth the only foundation on which the reason of man can repose. Philosophers, amidst all their efforts to break away from the common beliefs of mankind, have at last been compelled to come back to them as the only ultimate criterion of truth. "Fichte (says Sir W. Hamilton) is a more remarkable, because a more reluctant confessor to the paramount authority of belief than even Kant. Departing from the principle common to him, and philosophers in general, that the mind cannot transcend itself, Fichte developed, with the most admirable rigour of demonstration, a scheme of idealism the purest, simplest, and most consistent which the history of philosophy exhibits. And so confident was Fichte in the necessity of his proofs, that on one occasion he was provoked to imprecate eternal damnation on his head, should he ever swerve from any, even the least of the doctrines which he had so victoriously established. But even Fichte, in the end, confesses that natural belief is paramount to every logical proof, and that his own idealism he could not believe."

With the great fact before us, so triumphantly reclaimed and vindicated by Sir William Hamilton, that philosophers have never been able to find any other criterion of truth than the common sense of mankind, we will now proceed to show what is its doctrine.

The philosophy of common sense is the doctrine, in its development and applications, that our primary beliefs are the ultimate criterion of truth. It postulates, that consequents cannot, by an infinite regress, be evolved out of antecedents: but that demonstration must ultimately rest upon propositions which, in the view of certain primary beliefs of the mind, necessitate their own admission. These primary beliefs, as primary, must of course be inexplicable, being the highest light in the temple of mind, and borrowing no radiance from any higher cognition by which their own light can be illuminated. Behind these primary beliefs the mind cannot see—all is negation; because, while these primary beliefs are the first energy of the mind, they are also its limitation. The primary facts of intelligence would not be original, were they revealed to us under any other form than that of necessary belief.

As elements of our mental constitution, as essential conditions of intelligence itself, these primary beliefs *must*, at least in the first instance, be accepted as true. Else, we assume that the very root of our intelligence is a lie. All must admit some original bases of knowledge in the mind itself, and must *assume* that they are true.

The argument from common sense is therefore simply to show, that to deny a given proposition would involve a denial of a primary belief, an original datum of consciousness; and as the primary belief or original datum of consciousness must be received as veracious, the proposition necessitated by it must be received as true also.

It is manifest, that in arguing on the basis of our primary beliefs, they cannot be shown to be mendacious, unless it be demonstrated that they contradict each other, either immediately in themselves or mediately in their consequences. Because, there being no higher criterion by which to test their veracity, it can only be tested by agreement or contradiction between themselves.

We will now apply this doctrine, and in discussing the application, we will explicate the doctrine more fully. In the act of sensible perception we are, equally and at the same time, and in the same indivisible act of consciousness, cognizant of ourself as a perceiving subject, and of an external reality as the object perceived, which are apprehended as a synthesis inseparable in the cognition, but contrasted to each other in the concept as two distinct existences. All this is incontestably the deliverance of consciousness in the act of sensible perception. This all philosophers, without exception, admit as a *fact.* But then all, until Reid, deny the *truth* of the deliverance. They maintain that we only perceive representations within ourselves, and by a perpetual illusion we mistake these representations for the external realities. And Reid did not fully extricate himself from the trammels of this opinion. For while he repudiated the notion, that we perceive representations distinct from the mind though within the mind, he fell into the error, that we are only conscious of certain changes in ourselves which suggest the external reality. But Sir William Hamilton has, by the most masterly subtlety of analysis, incontestably shown, that we are directly conscious of the external objects themselves, according to the belief universal in the common sense of mankind.

It is manifest, that the whole question resolves itself into one of the veracity of consciousness. All admit that consciousness does testify to the *fact* that we perceive the external reality. To doubt this is to doubt the actuality of the fact of consciousness, and consequently to doubt the doubt itself, which is a contradiction, and subverts itself. The data then of consciousness, simply as *facts*, or *actual manifestations and deliverances*, cannot be denied without involving a contradiction; and therefore, the principle of contradiction, which we have shown is the only one to be applied to the solution of the question, recoils upon the skeptic himself, and makes doubt impossible. But then, the facts or deliverances of consciousness considered as *testimonies to the truth of facts beyond their own phenomenal reality*, are not altogether to be excluded from the domain of legitimate philosophical discussion. For this proposition by no means, like the other, involves a self-contradiction; and thereby repels even the possibility of doubt. Therefore philosophers, while they admit the fact of the testimony of consciousness, deny its *truth*. The dispute is not as to *what* is said, but as to the *truth* of what is said.

As, then, it has been admitted that the *fact* is an affirmation of our intelligent nature, its mendacity cannot be consistently assumed; for upon the principle of *falsus in uno, falsus in omnibus*, it would impeach the *fact* itself as an affirmation of nature, which we have shown involves a contradiction, and is therefore impossible. It is clear, then, that the burden of proof, in impeaching the absolute veracity of consciousness, lies upon those denying it. And as we have shown that the attempt to prove its mendacity has in all ages failed, and that all the most schismatic and skeptical have at last found repose for the struggling intellect only in the testimony of our primary beliefs, we are compelled by analysis, and by history, to acknowledge the doctrine of common sense the one catholic and perennial philosophy.

Here the question obtrudes itself into our view, *What is the logical significance of our primary beliefs?* and it is a question of paramount importance. Perhaps, in the answer to this question, we may differ from Sir William Hamilton; and therefore it is that we wish to signalize it.

It is implied in the doctrine of primary beliefs, that, at the root of every primordial act of the mind, there is a principle or law guaranteeing the procedure. For example, the initial act, from which induction starts, is guaranteed by such a principle or law of intelligence—*the principle of philosophical presumption.* Now, in order to distinguish these principles or laws from the universal truths which are generalized from individual truths of fact, they are called universal truths of intelligence. Now, we prefer to call these principles *laws* of intelligence, as more expressive of their real character, rather than *truths* of intelligence; because, in the operations of the mind, they are regulative and not cogitable, being in fact the poles on which thought turns. They are, in our thinking, silent in laws, rather than articulate in propositions.

We think that this is a discrimination that ought not to be slighted; and we venture to find fault that Sir William Hamilton uses the expressions, "fundamental facts," "beliefs," "primary propositions," "cognitions at first hand," as denoting the same primary data of consciousness, only from different points of view. We are not convinced of the propriety of his opinion implied in such various designations; and are constrained to believe that the confusing the distinction, which we have endeavoured to indicate, is the initial, the root of that cardinal heresy in philosophy which makes all cognition encentric—makes thought start out from a general notion native to the mind. We repudiate the doctrine that there ever is a belief or a cognition of the mind without its corresponding object. The deliverance of the primary and most incomprehensible belief is, *That its object is.* Thought never evades the fundamental antithesis of subject and object, which is the primary law of consciousness itself. In no instance is a notion, not even that of cause, time, or space, native to the mind, acquired from no adequate object, but purely subjective and regulative, imposing upon objective thought an illusive interpolation of itself.

We therefore, repeat, that our primary beliefs are not *within* consciousness as comprehended thought, but *in* consciousness as bases of thought. We cannot therefore assent, that, in different points of view, they may or may not be regarded as cognitions or propositions. We think they have not the equivocal character, which the ambiguous and various designations applied to them, by Sir William Hamilton, seem to us to indicate. They are but modes of one unifying consciousness, not rising, in degree of intellection, to cognitions.

But to call them "primary propositions," is what we chiefly object to. There are primary propositions, undoubtedly, which in the view of our primary beliefs, necessitate their own admission: but then, they are not to be confounded with the primary beliefs themselves. They are made up of a plurality of primary beliefs unified in a common conviction in consciousness, and articulated in language. The point of our objection is, to every form and semblance of the doctrine, *that all knowing is through previous knowledge* (which will be considered in the sequel), instead of merely through *the power of knowing.*

But to return from this digression: And while Sir William Hamilton thus points out the bases and the elements of truth, he exhibits the canons by which philosophical research is to be conducted. As Bacon, in the first book of the *Novum Organum*, exposed the sources of error in physical inquiry, and laid down precautionary rules for conducting future investigation, so Sir William Hamilton has enounced maxims for conducting the loftier and far more difficult research into our intellectual nature. And his philosophy is, in this particular, the consummation of that of Bacon. It explores the depths of consciousness, and educes those primary beliefs and fundamental laws of intelligence which Bacon merely assumed in his philosophy. Sir William Hamilton has lighted his torch at the lamps of both induction and deduction, and it burns with their combined light; and therefore it is, that he has been able to penetrate depths in the abysses of thought, which to Bacon and Aristotle were unfathomable darkness. How, in the spirit of Bacon, is the following admonition! "No philosopher has ever formally denied the truth, or disclaimed the authority of consciousness; but few or none have been content implicitly to accept, and consistently to follow out its dictates. Instead of humbly resorting to consciousness to draw from thence his doctrines and their proof, each dogmatic speculator looked only into consciousness, there to discover his preadopted opinions. In philosophy, men have abused the code of natural, as in theology, the code of positive revelation; and the epigraph of a great Protestant divine on the book of Scripture is certainly not less applicable to the book of consciousness :

> Hic liber est in quo quærit sua dogmata quisque;
> Invenit et pariter dogmata quisque sua."

And Hamilton, like Bacon, is not at all dismayed by the past failures in philosophy; but with the proud hopes of a great mind, conscious of the power of truth, he anticipates mighty triumphs in future for that philosophy which he has shown to have prevailed for more than two thousand years. "And yet (says he), although the past history of philosophy has, in a great measure, been only a history of variation and error; yet the cause of the variation being known, we obtain a valid ground of hope for the destiny of philosophy in future. Because, since philosophy has hitherto been inconsistent with itself, only in being inconsistent with the dictates of our natural beliefs—

> 'For Truth is catholic and Nature one;'—

it follows, that philosophy has simply to return to natural consciousness, to return to unity and truth.

"In doing this, we have only to attend to three maxims or precautions:

"1. That we admit nothing, not either an original datum of consciousness, or the legitimate consequence of such datum;

"2. That we embrace all the original data of consciousness, and all their legitimate consequences; and

"3. That we exhibit each of these in its individual integrity, neither disturbed nor mutilated, and in its relative place, whether of pre-eminence or subordination."

But Sir William does not stop his directions for investigation with these maxims. He gives marks, by which we can distinguish our original from our derivative convictions—by which we can determine what is, and what is not, a primary datum of consciousness. These marks or characters are four;—1st, *their incomprehensibility*—2d, *their simplicity*—3d, *their necessity* and *absolute universality*—4th, *their comparative evidence* and *certainty*. These characters are explicated by him, and rendered entirely capable of application to the purpose of analyzing thought into its elements.

But, besides these positive directions for ascertaining truth, Sir William Hamilton exposes the very roots of the false systems of philosophy which have prevailed in different times. As he shows, by the most searching analysis, that the philosophy of common sense has its root in the recognition of the absolute veracity of consciousness in sensible perception; so he shows, that all philosophical aberrations, or false systems of philosophy, have their respective roots either in a full or partial denial of its veracity. And he does not deal merely in generalities; but he articulately sets forth five great variations from truth and nature, which have prevailed as systems of philosophy, and shows the exact degree of rejection of the veracity of consciousness which constitutes the root of each. We are thereby enabled to see the roots of these great heresies laid bare, and can extirpate them, by the argument from common sense.

Such are the rules which Sir William Hamilton lays down for conducting inquiry in the province of mind. They are a development of the method of Bacon in its application to psychology, the highest branch of phenomenal philosophy.

We now approach a new development of the philosophy of common sense, called the philosophy of the conditioned. It constitutes the distinguishing feature of the philosophical system of Sir William Hamilton; and was developed by him to satisfy the needs of intelligence in combating the proud and vainglorious philosophy of Germany. It is a remarkable monument of the largeness, the profundity, and the penetrating acuteness of his intellect.

The philosophy of common sense assumes, that consciousness is the supreme faculty—in fact, that it is the complement of all the faculties—that what are called faculties are but acts of consciousness running into each other, and are not separated by those lines of demarcation which are imposed upon them by language for the needs of thinking about our intelligent nature. The supremacy of consciousness was the doctrine of Aristotle, of Des Cartes, and of Locke. Reid and Stewart reduced consciousness, in their system, to a special faculty only co-ordinate with the others. This heresy Sir William Hamilton, amongst his innumerable rectifications and developments of Reid's philosophy, has exposed, and by a singular felicity of analysis and explication, has restored consciousness to its rightful sovereignty over the empire of intelligence.

Having postulated that consciousness is the highest, and fundamental faculty of the human mind, it becomes necessary, in order to determine the nature of human knowledge, to determine the nature of consciousness.

Now, consciousness is only possible under the antithesis of the thinking mental self, and an object thought about, in correlation and limiting each other. It is, therefore, manifest, that knowledge, in its most fundamental and thoroughgoing analysis, is discriminated into two elements in contrast of each other.

These elements are appropriately designated, the *subject* and the *object*, the first applying to the conscious mind knowing, and the last, to that which is known. And all that pertains to the first is called *subjective*, and all that pertains to the last is called *objective*.

Philosophy is the science of knowledge. Therefore, philosophy must especially regard the grand and fundamental discrimination of the two primary elements of the *subjective* and *objective*, in any theory of knowledge it may propound.

Now, the first and fundamental problem, which presents itself in the science of knowledge is, *What can we know?* Upon the principles of the philosophy of common sense, the solution of the problem is found, by showing what are the conditions of our knowledge. These conditions, according to the thoroughgoing fundamental analysis of our knowledge just evinced, arise out of the nature of both of the two elements of our knowledge, the *subjective* and the *objective*.

Aristotle, who did so much towards analyzing human thought into its elements, strove also to classify all objects real under their ultimate identifications or categories in relation to thought. In modern times, Kant endeavoured to analyze intelligence into its ultimate elements in relation to its objects, and to show in these elements the basis of all thinking, and the guarantee of all certainty. Aristotle's categories, though extremely incomplete, and indeed, we may say bungling, as they confound derivative with simple notions, did something for correct thinking in pointing out, with more exactness, the relations of objects real to thought. But Kant, making a false division of intelligence itself into reason and understanding, blundered at the threshold, and while he analyzed reason into its supposed peculiar elements, to which he gave the Platonic name of Ideas, he analyzed understanding into its supposed peculiar elements, and gave them the Aristotelic name of Categories. Kant's analysis of our intelligence into its pure forms, made the human mind a fabric of mere delusion. The ideas of reason he proposed as purely subjective and regulative, and yet delusively positing themselves objectively in thought. And so too, in like manner, are his categories of understanding expounded as deceptive. His philosophy is thus rendered, at bottom, a system of absolute skepticism.

It is seen, from this account of them, that Aristotle's Categories or Predicaments are exclusively objective, of things understood; and that those of Kant are exclusively subjective, of the mind understanding. Each is therefore one-sided.

Sir William Hamilton, discriminating more accurately than his predecessors, the dual nature of thought, has distinguished its two fundamental elements, the subjective and the objective, by a thoroughgoing analysis, and at the same time has observed that these elements are ever held together in a synthesis which constitutes thought in its totality. He has therefore endeavoured to accomplish, in one analysis of thought, what Aristotle and Kant failed to do by their several but partial analyses. As thought is constituted of both a subjective and an objective element, the conditions of the thinkable or of thinking must be the conditions of both knowledge and existence—of the possibility of knowing, both from the nature of thought, and from the nature of existence; and must therefore embrace intelligence in relation to its objects, and objects in relation to intelligence, and thus supersede the one-sided predicaments of Aristotle and Kant.

The first step towards discriminating the fundamental conditions of thought, is to reduce thought itself to its ultimate simplicity. This Sir William Hamilton has done, by showing that it must be either positive or negative, when viewed subjectively, and either conditioned or unconditioned when viewed objectively. And he has discriminated, and signalized the peculiar nature of negative thought, by showing that it is conversant about the unconditioned, while positive thought is conversant about the conditioned. This is a salient point in Sir William's philosophy. He shows that the Kantean Ideas of pure reason are nothing but negations or impotences of the mind, and are swallowed up in the unconditioned; and that the

Kantean Categories of the understanding are but subordinate forms of the conditioned. And while he thus reduces the Predicaments of Kant to ultimate elements, he annihilates his division of our intelligence into reason and understanding. He shows that what Kant calls the reason is in fact an impotence, and what he calls the understanding is the whole intellect.

It had been shown by Aristotle, that negation involves affirmation—that non-existence can only be predicated by referring to existence. This discrimination has become a fruitful principle in the philosophy of Sir William Hamilton. He, therefore, begins the announcement of the conditions of the thinkable, by showing the nature of negative thought. He shows that negative thought is realized only under the condition of relativity and positive thinking. For example: we try to think—to predicate existence, and find ourselves unable. We then predicate incogitability. This incogitability is what is meant by negation or negative thought.

If then negative thinking be the opposite of positive thinking, it must be the violation of one or more of the conditions of positive thinking. The conditions of positive thinking are two; 1st. The condition of *non-contradiction:* 2d. The condition of *relativity.* To think at all (that is positively, for positive thinking is properly the only thinking), our thinking must not involve a contradiction, and it must involve relativity. If it involve contradiction, the impossible both in thought and in reality results. If the condition of relativity be not fulfilled, the impossible in thought only results.

Now the condition of non-contradiction is brought to bear in thinking under three phases constituting three laws:—1st. The law of *identity;* 2d. The law of *contradiction;* 3d. The law of *excluded middle.* The science of these laws is Logic. Thus is shown the ultimate condition of the thinkable on which depends the science of explicative or analytical reasoning. This we shall show fully in the sequel, when we come to treat of what Sir William Hamilton has done for Logic.

The condition of non-contradiction is in no danger of being violated in thinking; therefore its explication is only of theoretical importance.

The condition of relativity is the important one in thought. This condition, in so far as it is *necessary,* is brought to bear under two principal relations; one of which arises from the subjective element of thought, the mind thinking (called the *Relation of Knowledge*); the other arises from the objective element of thought, the thing thought about (called the *Relation of Existence*).

The relation of *Knowledge* arises from the reciprocal relation of the subject and the object of thought. Whatever comes into consciousness is thought, by us, as belonging to the mental self exclusively, or as belonging to the not-self exclusively, or as belonging partly to both.

The relation of *Existence* arising from the object of thought is two-fold: this relation being sometimes intrinsic, and sometimes extrinsic; according as it is determined by the qualitative or quantitative character of existence. Existence conceived as substance and quality, presents the intrinsic relation, called *qualitative;* substance and quality are only thought as mutual *relatives* inseparable in conception. We cannot think either separate from the other.

All that has thus far been said applies to both mind and matter.

The extrinsic relation of *Existence* is three-fold; and as constituted by three species of quantity, it may be called *quantitative.* It is realized in or by the three quantities, time, space, and degree, called respectively, protensive, extensive, and intensive quantity. The notions of time and space are the necessary conditions of all positive thought. Positive thought cannot be realized except in time and space. Degree is not, like time and space, an absolute condition of thought. Existence is not necessarily thought under degree. It applies only to quality and not to quantity; and only to quality, in a restricted sense which Sir William Hamilton has explicated in his doctrine of the qualities of bodies, dividing them into primary, secundo-primary, and secondary.

Of these conditions and their relations in their proper subordinations and co-ordinations Sir William has presented a table, which he calls the Alphabet of Thought.

Out of the condition of relativity springs the science of metaphysics, just as we have indicated that logic springs out of the condition of non-contradiction. Thus the respective roots of the two great cognate branches of philosophy are traced to their psychological bases in the alphabet of thought.

We will now exhibit the metaphysical doctrine, which Sir William Hamilton educes from the analysis of thought which we have endeavoured to present. And here he elevates the philosophy of common sense into the philosophy of the conditioned, borrowing this appellation from the different point of view from which philosophy is considered. The former appellation is derived from a psychological point of view, the latter from a metaphysical—the former from a subjective, the latter from an objective.

It is sufficiently apparent that the condition of relativity limits our knowledge. This is the fundamental fact which it is proposed to establish. It is proposed to show that of the absolute we have no knowledge, but only of the relative. This is the whole scope of the philosophy of the conditioned.

With a view of showing the argument from the philosophy of the conditioned, let us turn, for a moment, to the philosophy of the absolute, the unconditioned, which is the reverse doctrine, and for the refutation of which the conditions of the thinkable are adduced as a basis.

From the dawn of philosophy in the school of Elea, the absolute, the infinite, the unconditioned, has been the highest principle of speculation. The great master amongst ancient philosophers, Aristotle, in accordance with the general drift of his philosophy, denied that the Infinite is even an object of thought, much less of knowledge. And that profound, and subtle, but perverse and paradoxical genius, Kant, who, towards the close of the eighteenth century, made the first serious attempt ever made, to investigate the nature and origin of the notion of the Infinite, maintained that the notion is merely regulative of our thoughts; and declared the Infinite to be utterly beyond the sphere of our knowledge. But out of the philosophy of Kant, from a hidden germ, grew a more extravagant theory of the absolute than any which had before perplexed and astounded the practical reason of man. It was maintained by Fichte and Schelling—who fell back on the ancient notion, that experience, because conversant only about the phenomenal and transitory, is unworthy of the name of philosophy as incapable of being a valid basis of certainty and knowledge—that man has a faculty of *intellectual intuition* which rises above the sphere of consciousness, as well as of sense, and enthroning the reason of man on the seat of Omniscience, with which it in fact becomes identified, surveys existence in its all-comprehensive unity and its all-pervading relations, and unveils to us the nature of God, and, by an ontological evolution, explains the derivation of all things, from the greatest to the very least.

This philosophy captivated the brilliant and sympathetic genius of M. Cousin, of France, who strove to conciliate and harmonize it with the Scottish philosophy of experience as promulgated by Reid, with which M. Cousin had been imbued. He denied the *intellectual intuition* of the German philosophers, and claimed that the Infinite is given as a datum in consciousness along with its correlative the Finite; that these two notions, being necessarily thought as mutual relatives, must therefore be both equally objectively true. These two notions and their relations to each other are, at once, the elements and the laws of the reason of both man and God, and that all this is realized in and through consciousness. This theory M. Cousin proclaimed as a powerful eclecticism, which conciliated not only what had been before considered counter and hostile in the reflections of individual philosophers, but also, in the different systems of philosophy preserved in the history of the science. Thus, the history of philosophy, with its various systems, was shown to be but the growth of one regularly developed philosophy, gradually culminating towards that one consummate knowledge completed in the all-comprehending eclecticism inaugurated, in the central nation of Europe, by M. Cousin in a splendour of discourse worthy of the grand doctrine which makes the proud rationalism of Germany acknowledge its doctrinal affiliation with the humble Scottish philosophy of observation. When this doctrine reached Scotland, Sir William Hamilton, at once, entered the great olympic of philosophical discussion, and stood forth, as the champion of the humble doctrine of common sense, against the host of continental thinkers.

And now, for the first time in the history of philosophy, the doctrine of the Absolute, the Infinite, the Unconditioned, was made definite. It was shown, by Sir William Hamilton, that so far from the Absolute and the Infinite meaning the same thing or notion, they were contradictory opposites; the Absolute meaning the unconditional affirmation of limitation, while the Infinite means the unconditional negation of limitation—the one thus an affirmative, the other a negative. And he further showed, that both were but species of the unconditioned. The question being thus purified from the inaccuracy of language and the confusion of thought; and it being shown that the unconditioned must present itself to the human mind in a plural form; it was seen that the inquiry resolves itself into the problem, whether the unconditioned, as either the Absolute or the Infinite can be realized to the mind of man. Sir William Hamilton shows that it cannot. He demonstrates that in order to think either alternative, we must think away from those conditions of thought under which thought can alone be realized; and that, therefore, any attempt to think either the Absolute or the Infinite must end in a mere negation of thought. These notions are thus shown to be the results of two counter imbecilities of the mind—the inability to realize the unconditionally limited, and the unconditionally unlimited. The doctrine of M. Cousin is shown to be assumptious, inconsequent, and self-contradictory. His Infinite is shown to be, at best, only an Indefinite, and therefore a relative. And it is shown, by a comprehensive application of the Aristotelic doctrine, that the knowledge of opposites is one, that so far from the fact, of the notions of the Infinite and Finite mutually suggesting each other, furnishing evidence of the objective reality of both, it should create a suspicion of the reverse. The truth is, the searching analysis, to which the doctrine of M. Cousin is subjected, clearly evinces that he did not at all apprehend the state of the question discussed, and in fact was confusing himself in a vicious circle of words.

And the *Intellectual Intuition* of Fichte and Schelling is shown to be a mere chimera; and their Absolute, a mere nothing. As Schelling could never connect his Absolute with the Finite in any doctrinal affiliation, so he was unable to discover any cognitive transition from the Intellectual Intuition to personal consciousness. This hiatus in his theory could not, of course, escape the penetrating sagacity of Sir William Hamilton. It was at once demonstrated as the Intellectual Intuition is out of and above consciousness, and to be realized, the philosopher must cease to be the conscious man Schelling, that if even the Intellectual Intuition were possible, still it could only be remembered, and *ex hypothesi*, it could not be remembered, for memory is only possible under the conditions of the understanding which exclude the Absolute from knowledge. By this analysis the Absolute is shown to be a mere mirage in the infinite desert of negation, conjured up by a self-delusive imagination, conceiting itself wise above the possibilities of thought. It may also be argued against the Intellectual Intuition, that it is only through the organism of sense, that the mind realizes *form*, the image of an object; for consciousness in and of itself is not an imaging faculty. Now the Intellectual Intuition realizes *image* in the Absolute. It therefore partakes of the character of sensation; and it, in fact, by this analysis stands revealed as a sublimated sense postulated, by reason overleaping itself, in the attempt to clear the circle of the thinkable. The doctrine of the Absolute is thus proved to be a sensational philosophy, disguised under terms of supposed high spiritual import. And thus, it is demonstrated, that to abandon consciousness as the highest faculty, is to necessitate a fall into sensuism, though we imagine, all the while, we are soaring on the wings of reason, above the region of consciousness. Schelling and Condillac are thus found in the darkness of a common error listening to the same oracle. And this analysis is confirmed, by the fact, that Oken, who, next to Hegel, was the most distinguished disciple of Schelling, in his Physio-Philosophy, makes the Absolute *nothing*, zero; and then, by pure reason, evolves, out of it, all physics; thus ascribing to a faculty, above consciousness, the imaging power of the senses. And Oken thus enthrones the physical sciences, as he imagines, on a seat above consciousness, when it is, in fact, the footstool of consciousness, the senses, on which they sit the while.*

* It is true that Schelling makes the manner of knowing the absolute presentative, by the fiction of an intellectual intuition emancipated from the conditions of time and space, while Hegel makes this manner of knowing representative, by the fiction of a logical reason emancipated from the laws of thought. Yet I am right in saying that the intellectual intuition, if possible, must possess an imaging power and therefore is sensational; because in knowing the absolute, imagination and conception must concur, for the absolute must be considered individual.

Thus was trampled down, this proud doctrine which had misled speculation; and philosophy was again brought back from its aberrations into the sober paths of common sense. And never before did so mighty a champion lead it. For whatever else may be thought, in comparing Sir William Hamilton with other philosophers, it must he admitted that as a man of hostilities, a dialectician and a critic, he is altogether matchless.

Having given an all-comprehensive example of the argument from the philosophy of the conditioned, we will now proceed to expound, in outline, the philosophy of the conditioned. The distinguishing feature of this philosophy, the one which most articulately enounces its character, is the doctrine of a mental *Impotence.* This doctrine we will now expound.

The problem most fruitful of controversy in philosophy is that of the distinction between experiential and non-experiential notions and judgments. Some philosophers contend that there is no such distinction; but that all legitimate notions and judgments are experiential. And those who have admitted the distinction have quarrelled about the criterion of the distinction. Leibnitz, at last, established the quality of *necessity*, the neces-

---

It may be said, however, that the intellectual intuition assumes that both conception and imagination do not belong to its manner of knowing. This is only further evidence that it is a fiction.

sity of so thinking, as the criterion of our non-experiential notions and judgments. Afterwards Kant, in his Critic of Pure Reason, developed and applied this criterion. And it may now be considered as the acknowledged test of our unacquired cognitions amongst those who admit that there are non-experiential notions and judgments. Now, it is in relation to this fundamental distinction, that Sir William Hamilton has developed the philosophy of the conditioned. He admits that we have non-experiential notions and judgments (we prefer to call the two classes of notions and judgments, *primary* and *secondary*, as we think both classes, from a certain point of view, can appropriately be considered as experiential in a restricted sense), and he concurs with Leibnitz and Kant, that *necessity* is their distinctive quality. But then, he maintains that the doctrine, as developed by all previous philosophers, is one-sided, when it should be two-sided. And the side of the doctrine, which philosophers have overlooked, is the important one. The doctrine, as heretofore enounced and recognized, is that the necessity is a positive one, *so to think*, and is determined by a mental power. But Sir William Hamilton considers, and very justly, that this is only half of the truth, and the least important half; because this necessity is never illusive, never constrains to error; while the necessity which he indicates is naturally illusive. His doctrine is, that this necessity is both positive and negative: "The one, the necessity of so thinking (the impossibility of *not so* thinking), determined by a mental power, the other the necessity of *not so* thinking (the impossibility of *so* thinking), determined by a mental impotence." This negative necessity, which has been overlooked by philosophers, plays an important part on the theatre of thinking. It is to the development of its function in our mental economy, that the philosophy of the conditioned is directed. As philosophy stood, the very highest law of intelligence, which asserts that of two contradictories, both cannot, but one must, be true, led continually to the most pervasive and fundamental errors. Because when one alternative was found incogitable, the mind immediately recoiled to the conclusion that the other contradictory must be true. When, for example, in examining the doctrine of the will, it was discovered that the freedom of the will was incomprehensible, could not be speculatively construed to the mind, the inquirer immediately recoiled to the alternative, of the necessity of human actions; and so on the other hand, when the necessity of the will was found incogitable, the inquirer fell back upon the alternative of liberty. So that philosophers, like Milton's fallen angels, had

> ". . . . . . . . . . . reasoned high
> Of Providence, foreknowledge, will, and fate,
> Fixt fate, freewill, foreknowledge absolute,
> And found no end, in wandering mazes lost."

Thus the negative necessity, of *not so thinking*, which was not ever even suspected to exist, had been a source of constant errors utterly incapable of solution. But Sir William Hamilton has discovered, that we may be negatively unable to think one contradictory, and yet find ourselves equally impotent to conceive the opposite. To this fundamental psychological fact he has applied the highest law of intelligence, *that of two contradictories, one must of necessity be true;* and that therefore, there is no ground for inferring a fact to be impossible, merely from our inability to conceive its possibility. And thus is disclosed the hidden rock on which speculation, in its highest problems, had foundered.

The philosophy of the conditioned is the development and application of this Negative Necessity in combination with the Positive. In order to give precision to the doctrine of the conditioned, the conditions of the thinkable are evoked and systematized under the two fundamental categories of positive and negative thinking. And these categories are themselves subdivided in order to bring out their import in generic instances of their application in practical thought. These conditions of the thinkable we have exhibited; but it now becomes necessary to recur to them, for the needs of the discussion and exposition on which we now enter.

The most important and comprehensive question in metaphysics is, *The origin and nature of the causal judgment.* No less than seven theories had been propounded on the problem; and now, Sir William Hamilton has propounded an eighth, entirely new. He attempts to resolve the causal judgment into a modification of the law of the conditioned, which is so obtrusive in his view of philosophy. He makes the causal judgment a mere inability to think an absolute beginning:—a mere necessity to deny that the object, which we apprehend as beginning to be, really so begins:—an inability to construe it in thought, as possible, that the complement of existence has been increased or diminished:—a mere necessity to affirm the identity of its present sum of being, with the sum of its past existence. The supposed connection between cause and effect is in its last analysis, resolved into a mental impotence, the result of the law of the conditioned.

It is manifest, that in this theory, the fact of our inability to conceive the complement of existence, either increased or diminished, is the turning point in the question. That, because we are unable to construe it, in thought, that such increase or diminution is possible, we are constrained to refund the present sum of existence into the previous sum of existence, is given as an explanation of the causal judgment.

Now, it seems to us that this solution avoids the important element in the phenomenon to be explained. The question in nature, is not whether the present complement of existence had a previous existence—has just begun to be? but, how comes its new appearance? The obtrusive and essential element, is the *new appearance*, the *change*. This is the fact which elicits the causal judgment. To the *change* is necessarily prefixed, by the understanding, a cause or potence. The cause is the correlative to the change, elicited in thought and posited in nature. The question as to the origin of the sum of existence, does in no way intrude into consciousness, and is not involved in the causal judgment. Such a question may, of course, be raised; and then the theory of Sir William Hamilton is a true account of what would take place in the mind. And this is the question, which, it seems to us, Sir William has presented as the problem of the causal judgment. His statement of the problem is this: "When aware of a *new* appearance, we are *unable* to conceive that therein has originated any new existence, and are therefore constrained to think that what now appears to us under a new form, had previously an existence under others—others conceivable by us or not. We are utterly unable to construe it in thought, as possible that the complement of existence has been increased or diminished."

This seems to us, not a proper statement of the problem of causation. This problem does not require the *complement of existence* to be accounted for; but the *new form* to be accounted for; and a new form must not be confounded with an *entirely new existence*.

Causation must be discriminated from creation; in the first, *change* only, in the last, the *complement of existence,* is involved. If we attempt to solve the problem of *creation,* the notion of an absolute beginning is involved; consequently, a negative impotence is experienced, as we cannot think an absolute beginning, and we would fall back on the notion of causation—would stop short at the causal judgment, unable to rise to a higher cognition—the cognition of creation.

The causal judgment consists in the necessity we are under of prefixing in thought a cause to every change, of which we think. Now change implies previous existence; else it is not change. Of what does it imply the previous existence? Of that which is changed, and also of that by which the change is effected. Now change is effect. It is the result of an operation. Operation is cause (potence) realizing itself in effect. It seems to us, by this somewhat tautological analysis, that cause and effect necessarily imply each other, both in nature and in thought. Causality is thought both as a law of things and a law of intelligence. When we attempt to separate effect from cause, in our thought, contradiction emerges. It is realized to consciousness in every act of will, and in every act of positive thinking as both natural and rational. Cause and effect are related to each other, as terms in thought, as well as realities in existence.

Causality is primarily natural, secondarily rational. The woof of reasoning, into which its notion is woven, has the two threads of the material and the rational running together, by which existence and thought are harmonized into truth; the objective responding to the subjective. If this were not the law of material thinking, we do not see how there could be any consecutive thinking about nature. The notion of cause always leads thought in material reasoning—always determines the mental conclusion, as the notion of reason does in formal or pure reasoning. The law of cause and effect is, in material thought, what the law of reason and consequent is in formal thought.

It is doubtless true, that the negative impotence to think an absolute beginning necessarily connects in thought present with past existence; and as all change must take place in some existence, the change itself is connected in thought with something antecedent; and, therefore, the mind is necessitated by the negative impotence to predicate something antecedent to the change. But, then, as a mere negative impotence cannot yield an affirmative judgment, it cannot connect present with past existence, in the relation of cause and effect, but only in sum of existence which it is unable to think either increased or diminished. The causal judgment is determined by a mental power elicited into action by an observed change, and justified thereby as an affirmation of a potence evinced in the changed existence; and it matters not whether the change be the result of many concurring causes, or of one; still the notion of potence cannot but be thought as involved in the phenomenon. When we see a tree shivered to atoms by a flash of lightning, it is difficult to be convinced, that the causal judgment elicited by the phenomenon, is merely the impotence to think an absolute beginning.

We are conscious that we are the authors of our own actions; and this is, to be conscious of causation in ourselves. But if we attempt to analyze this fact in consciousness by considering it as made up of two elements related in time, we confuse ourselves by the impotence to conceive any causal nexus between the supposed antecedent and consequent. The fact is, that they are a simultaneous deliverance of consciousness realizing an antithesis in one inseparable act; because cause and effect are never realized separately, but conjointly. Efficiency is twofold, partly cause, partly effect, and cannot be thought otherwise without contradiction. Cause is thus thought as an indefinite, as not having either an absolute beginning or ending. Absolute beginning is not more necessary to the notion of cause than to that of time. Both are thought as quantities, and though both are thought as indeterminates, like all indeterminates, are capable of a determinate application. And while realized as particular, they are thought as universal.

We are prone to postulate principles more absolutely than they are warranted by nature. Therefore it is, that the subtleties of nature so often drop through the formulas of the logician; and he retains in their stead abstractions not corresponding with existence. Excessive study of formal logic tends to lessen the capacity for appreciating the imports of intuition. The apodictic character of logical relations is so different from that of mere material relations, that a mind, long addicted to the estimation of the former, cannot but contract a fallacious bias somewhat like that of the mere analytical mathematician, but of course to a much less degree. And on the other hand, a metaphysician, who like Locke, is deficient in a knowledge of logic, and unpractised in its precise distinctions and forms, becomes loose, inconsequent, and contradictious in his opinions. We venture to suggest, that the former of these biases is apparent in the application of the law of the conditioned to the causal judgment, by Sir William Hamilton. He postulates it too unqualifiedly.

The doctrine of the conditioned rescues thought from otherwise insoluble contradictions, by carrying up the contradictory phenomena into a common principle of limitation of our faculties. For example: If we attempt to think an absolute beginning, we find it impossible; and on the other hand, if we attempt to think its contradictory opposite, an infinite non-beginning, we find it equally incogitable. If therefore, both be received as positive affirmative deliverances of our intelligence, then our minds testify, by necessity, to lies. But the philosophy of the conditioned emphatically forbids us to confound, as equivalent, non-existence with incogitability; because it does not make the human mind the measure of existence, but just the reverse. It postulates as its fundamental principle, that the incogitable may and must be necessarily true upon the acknowledged highest principle of intelligence, that of two contradictories one must, but both cannot be true. Thus by carrying up these contradictions into the common principle of a limitation of our faculties, intelligence is shown to be feeble, but not false; and the contradictory phenomena are rescued from contradiction, by showing that one must be true. And by this doctrine, the moral responsibility of man is vindicated from all cavil. Thus while the liberty of the will is inconceivable, so is its contradictory opposite, the necessity of human actions. As then, these two negations are at equipoise, and can neither prove nor disprove anything, the testimony of consciousness, that we are, though we know not how, the real and responsible authors of our actions, gives the affirmance to our accountability. And out of this moral germ springs the root of the argument for the existence of

God, which combined with the lately too much disparaged argument from design,* constitutes a valid basis for the doctrine of natural Theology. Thus are vindicated, by this new development of the philosophy of common sense, the great truths of our practical reason, as they have been called; and speculation and practice are reconciled. And the doctrine that God is incognizable is demonstrated; and that it is only through the analogy of the human with the divine nature, that we are percipient of the existence of God. Power and knowledge, and virtue cognized in ourselves, and tending to consummation, reveal the notion of God. For unless all analogy be rejected, the mind must *believe* in that first cause, which by the limited nature of our faculties we cannot *know*. In the language of the great Puritan divine, John Owen: "All the rational conceptions of the minds of men are swallowed up and lost, when they would exercise themselves directly on that which is absolutely immense, eternal, infinite. When we say it is so, we know not what we say, but only that it is not otherwise. What we *deny* of God we know in some measure—but what

* The evidences of design in nature have, in all ages and with all orders of minds, done more to uphold natural, or rational theology than all other evidences put together. The argument founded in our moral nature, so much in vogue with those who aspire to the subtleties of Kant, is wholly incompetent without the argument from design to corroborate it.

we *affirm* we know not; only we declare what we *believe* and adore."

While therefore, this philosophy confines *our knowledge* to the conditioned, it leaves *faith* free about the unconditioned; indeed constrains us to believe in it, by the highest law of our intelligence. This fundamental truth of his philosophy Sir William Hamilton has enounced in this comprehensive canon: "Thought is possible only in the conditioned interval between two unconditioned contradictory extremes or poles, each of which is altogether inconceivable, but of which, on the principle of Excluded Middle, the one or the other is necessarily true." As therefore the unconditioned, as we have seen, presents itself to the human mind, under a plural form of contradictory opposites, as either the absolute or the infinite, the problem comes under this canon, and the unconditioned is established as a verity, incognizable but *believable.* Thus, in the very fact of the limitation of our knowledge, is discovered the affirmation, by the highest law of our intelligence, of the transcendent nature of faith. There is no philosophy, which in its spirit, its scope, and its doctrines, both positive and negative, so conciliates and upholds revealed religion, as that which is based on this great canon of Metaphysics. The conditions on which revelation with its complement of doctrines, is offered to our belief, are precisely those which this canon enounces.

Having exhibited an outline of what Sir William Hamilton has done for Metaphysics, we will now proceed to show what he has done for Logic.

In what we have said about the relation, which the philosophy of Sir William Hamilton bears to that of Bacon, we, by no means, intend to affirm, that there is much intellectual sympathy between the two great thinkers. It is quite otherwise. Bacon was pre-eminently objective, exhausting his great powers chiefly in the field of physics, because, in his time, there lay the needs of truth; while Hamilton, rather turning his back on physics, because of their now extravagant cultivation, is supremely subjective, throwing his vast energies upon inquiries in the province of intellectual philosophy. And though Sir William Hamilton does not directly disparage the labours of Bacon, yet he vaunts those of Des Cartes at their expense, and certainly nowhere does those of Bacon justice. But still the philosophies of Bacon and of Hamilton are concordant developments of the one philosophy of common sense, and are affiliated in unity of fundamental doctrine. Bacon is the forerunner, in that great intellectual movement, to which Hamilton has communicated such a mighty energy of thought, contributed the light of such vast erudition, and adduced such stringent historical proofs of its perennial existence. It is the inductive branch of Logic with its kindred doctrines, which Sir William Hamilton has brought out into bold relief, from the subordination in which it was held by Aristotle: while, at the same time, he has so developed and simplified by a completer analysis, the deductive branch, that the Stagirite only retains his superior fame by being the precursor. And it is, by his successful labours upon these two great branches of Logic, that Sir William Hamilton conciliates the philosophies of Aristotle and Bacon; and gives to modern thought a force of reasoning, through the practical application of nicer discriminations of the forms of thought, and more adequate logical expression, which elevates this century to a higher intellectual platform. All this shall sufficiently appear in the sequel.

When, in the year 1833, Sir William Hamilton published in the Edinburgh Review, his criticism on Whately's Logic, there was prevalent in Britain, total ignorance of the higher logical philosophy. The treatise of Whately was the highest logical standard; which, though in ability it is much above mediocrity, in erudition is far below the literature of the subject. The article of Sir William elevated the views of British logicians above the level of Whately, and gave them glimpses of a higher doctrine. But the chief service rendered by this masterly criticism, was the precision with which it defined the nature and the object matter of logic, and discriminated the whole subject doctrinally and historically, in the concentrated light of its literature.

The treatise of Whately presents indistinct, ambiguous and even contradictory views of the proper object matter of logic. Sometimes it makes the process or operation of reasoning, the total matter about which logic is conversant; at other times, it makes logic entirely conversant about language. Now, though it involves a manifest contradiction to say, that logic is exclusively conversant about each of two opposite things, yet Whately was praised by British logicians for the clearness with which he displayed the true nature and office of logic. In the low state of logical knowledge in Britain, which these facts indicate, it behooved whoever undertook to point out Whately's blunders to enter into the most elementary discussion of logic, both name and thing. This Sir William Hamilton did in the article now under consideration.

Aristotle designated logic by no single term. He employed different terms to designate particular parts or applications of logic; as is shown by the names of his several treatises. In fact, Aristotle did not look at logic from any central point of view. And, indeed, his treatises are so overladen with extralogical matter, as to show that the true theoretical view of logic as an independent science had not disclosed itself to its great founder. In fact, it has only been gradually, that the proper view of the science has been speculatively adopted—practically it never has been; and no contribution to the literature of the subject has done so much to discriminate the true domain of logic, as this article of Sir William Hamilton. It marks an era in the science. Mounting up to the father of logic himself, it showed that nineteen-twentieths of his logical treatises, treat of matters that transcend logic considered as a formal science. It is shown that the whole doctrine of the modality of syllogisms does not belong to logic; for if any matter, be it demonstrative or probable, be admitted into logic, none can be excluded. And thus, with the consideration of the *real truth or falsehood* of propositions, the whole body of *real* science must come within the domain of logic, obliterating all distinction between *formal* and *real* inference.

The doctrine maintained in this article is, that logic is conversant about the laws of thought considered merely as thought. The import of this doctrine we will now attempt to unfold. The term *thought* is used in several significations of very different extent. It is sometimes used to designate every mental modification of which we are conscious, including will, feeling, desire. It is sometimes used in the more limited sense of every *cognitive* fact, excluding will, feeling, desire. In its most limited meaning, it denotes only the acts of the understanding or faculty of comparison or relation, called also the discursive or elaborative faculty. It is in this most restricted sense that the word *thought* is used in relation to logic. Logic supposes the materials of thought already in the mind, and only considers the manner of their elaboration. And the operation of the elaborative faculty on these materials is what is meant by *thought proper*. And it is the laws of thought, in this, its restricted sense, about which logic is conversant.

It must be further discriminated, that logic is conversant about thought as a product, and not about the producing operation or process; this belongs to psychology. Logic, therefore, in treating of the laws of thought, treats of them in regard to thought considered as a product. What, then, is thought? In other words, what are the acts of the elaborative faculty? They are three, conception, judgment, reasoning. These are all acts of comparison—gradations of thought. Of these, as producing acts, psychology treats. Logic treats of the products of these, called respectively, a concept, a judgment, a reasoning. The most articulate enunciation, therefore, of the intrinsic nature of logic is, *the science of the formal laws of thought considered as a product, and not as a process.*

But we will show still further what a form of thought is. In an act of thinking there are three things, which we can discriminate in consciousness. First, there is a thinking subject; second, an object which we think, called the matter of thought; and third, the relation subsisting between the subject and object of which we are conscious—a relation always manifested in some mode or manner. This last is the form of thought.

Now logic takes account only of this last—the form of thought. In so far as the form of thought is viewed in relation to the subject, as an act, operation, or energy, it belongs to psychology. It is only in reference to what is thought about, only considered as a product, that the form of the act, or operation, or energy, has relation to logic.

With this explanation, we will now enounce the laws of thought, of which logic is the science.

In treating of the conditions of the thinkable, as systematized by Sir William Hamilton, we have pointed out the fact, that it is shown, that logic springs out of the condition of non-contradiction; for that this condition is brought to bear only under three phases constituting three laws: 1st, the law of *Identity;* 2d, the law of *Contradiction;* 3d, the law of *Excluded Middle:* of which laws logic is the science. Of these laws we will treat in their order, and explicate the import or logical significance of each.

The principle of *Identity* expresses the relation of total sameness, in which, a product of the thinking faculty, be it concept, judgment, or reasoning, stands to all, and the relation of partial sameness, in which it stands to each, of its constituent characters. This principle is the special application of the absolute equivalence of the whole and its parts taken together, applied to the thinking of a thing, by the attribution of its constituent or distinctive characters. In the predicate the whole is contained explicitly, and in the subject implicitly. The logical significance of the law lies in this—that it is the principle of all logical affirmation—of all logical definition.

The second law, that of *Contradiction*, is this: What is contradictory is unthinkable. Its principle may be thus expressed: When a concept is determined by the attribution or affirmation of a certain character, mark, note, or quality, the concept cannot be thought to be the same when such character is denied of it. Assertions are mutually contradictory, when the one affirms that a thing possesses, or is determined by, the characters which the other affirms it does not possess or is not determined by. The logical significance of this law consists in its being the principle of all logical negation, or distinction.

The laws of *Identity* and *Contradiction* are co-ordinate and reciprocally relative: and neither can be deduced from the other; for each supposes the other.

The third law, called the principle of *Excluded Middle*, embraces that condition of thought which compels us, of two contradictory notions (which cannot both exist by the law of contradiction), to think either the one or the other as existing. By the laws of *Identity* and *Contradiction*, we are warranted to conclude from the truth of one contradictory to the falsehood of the other; and by the law of *Excluded Middle*, we are warranted to conclude from the falsehood of one, to the truth of the other. The logical significance of this law consists in this—that it determines that, of two forms given in the laws of *Identity* and *Contradiction*, and by these laws affirmed as those exclusively possible, that of these two only possible forms, the one or the other must be affirmed, as necessary, of every object. This law is the principle of disjunctive judgments, which stand in such mutual relation, that the affirmation of the one is the denial of the other.

These three laws stand to each other in relation like the three sides of a triangle. They are not the same, not reducible to unity, yet each giving, in its own existence, that of the other. They form one principle in different aspects.

These laws are but phases of that condition of the thinkable which stipulates for the absolute absence of contradiction. Whatever, therefore, violates these laws is impossible not only in thought but in existence; and they thus determine, for us, the sphere of possibility and impossibility, not merely in thought but in reality. They are therefore not wholly logical but also metaphysical. To deny the universal application of these laws is to subvert the reality of thought; and as the subversion would be an act of thought, it annihilates itself. They are therefore insuperable.

There is a fourth law which is a corollary of these three primary laws, called the law of *Reason* and *Consequent*, which is so obtrusive in our reasoning that it needs to be specially considered. The logical significance of this law lies in this, that in virtue of it, thought is constituted into a series of acts indissolubly connected, each necessarily inferring the other. The mind is necessitated to this or that determinate act of thinking, by a knowledge of something different from the thinking process itself. That which determines the mind is called the reason, that to which the mind is determined is called the consequent, and the relation between the two is called the consequence. By reason of our intelligent nature, there is a necessary dependence of one notion upon another, from which all logical inference results as an inevitable consequent. This inference is of two kinds. It must proceed, from the whole to the parts, or from the parts to the whole. When the determining notion (the reason) is conceived as a whole *containing* (under it) and therefore necessitating the determined notion (the consequent) conceived as its *contained part* or *parts*, argumentation proceeds, by mental analysis, from the whole to the parts into which it is separated. When the determining notion is conceived as the *parts constituting*, and therefore necessitating the determined notion conceived as the constituted whole, argumentation proceeds, by mental synthesis, from the parts to the whole. The process from the whole to the parts is called deductive reasoning; the other process, from the parts to the whole, is called inductive reasoning. There is therefore in logic a deductive syllogism and an inductive syllogism. The former is governed by the rule:—*What belongs (or does not belong) to the containing whole, belongs (or does not belong) to each and all of the contained parts.* The latter by the rule:—*What belongs (or does not belong) to all the constituent parts, belongs (or does not belong) to the constituted whole.* These rules exclusively determine all formal inference; whatever transcends or violates them, transcends or violates logic.

Sir William Hamilton was the first to discriminate accurately the difference between the deductive and inductive syllogism. All that had been said by logicians, except Aristotle, and he is brief, and by no means unambiguous, on logical induction, is entirely erroneous; for they all, including Whately, confound logical or formal induction, with that which is philosophical, and material, and extralogical. They consider logical induction not as governed by the necessary laws of thought, but as determined by the probabilities of the sciences from which the matter is borrowed. All inductive reasoning logical and material proceeds from the parts (singulars) to the whole (universal): but in the formal or subjective, the illation is different from that in the material or objective. In the former, the illation is founded on the necessary laws of thought; in the latter, on the general or particular analogies of nature. The logician knows no principle, but the necessary laws of thought. His conclusions are necessitated, not presumed.

All this confusion was produced by the introduction into formal logic of various kinds of matter. Aristotle himself corrupted logic in this way, and Sir William Hamilton has been the first to expel entirely this foreign element, and to purify logic from the resulting errors, though Kant had done much toward the same result. When we reflect that the only legitimate illation in formal logic is that regulated by the law of reason and consequent, which connects thought into a reciprocally dependent series, each necessarily inferring the other, it is at once manifest that the distinction of matter into possible, actual, and necessary, is a doctrine wholly extralogical. Logical illation never differs in degree—never falls below that of absolute necessity. The necessary laws of thought constraining an inevitable illation, are the only principle known to the logician.

We have just seen that Sir William Hamilton is the first to signalize the fact, that reasoning from the parts to the whole is just as necessary, and exclusive of material considerations, as reasoning from the whole to the parts. And he has evolved the laws of the Inductive Syllogism, and correlated them with those of the Deductive Syllogism.

We now proceed to another important addition which he has made to logic. He has shown that there are two logical wholes, instead of one, as the logicians had supposed. These two wholes are the whole of Comprehension, called by Sir William, Depth, and the whole of Extension, called by him Breadth. These two wholes are in an inverse ratio of each other. The maximum of depth and the minimum of breadth are found in the concept of an individual (which in reality is not a concept, but only a single representation); while the minimum of breadth and the maximum of depth is found in a simple concept—the concept of being or existence. Now, the depth of notions affords one or two branches of reasoning, which, though overlooked by logicians, is at least equally important as that afforded by their breadth, which alone has been developed by the logicians. The character of the former is that the predicate is contained *in the subject;* of the latter, that the subject is *contained under* the predicate. All reasoning, therefore, is either from the whole to the parts, or from the parts to the whole, in breadth; or from the whole to the parts, or from the parts to the whole, in depth. The quantity of breadth is the creation of the mind, the quantity of depth is at once given in the very nature of things. The former, therefore, is factitious, the latter is natural. The same proposition forms a different premise in these different quantities, they being inverse ratios; the Sumption in Breadth being the Subsumption in Depth.

Another fundamental development of logic made by Sir William, is that the Categorical Syllogism, though mentally one (for all mediate inference is one and that categorical), is either Analytic or Synthetic, from the necessity of adopting the one order or the other, in compliance with that condition of language which requires that a reasoning be distinguished into parts and detailed in order of sequence. Because explication is sometimes better attained by an analytic and sometimes by a synthetic enouncement; as is shown in common language. The Aristotelic syllogism is exclusively synthetic. Sir William Hamilton thus relieves the syllogism from a one-sided view, and also rescues it from the objection of *Petitio Principii* or of an idle tautology, which has been so often urged against it. Such objection does not hold against the analytic syllogism, in which the conclusion is expressed first, and the premises are then stated as its reasons. And this form of reasoning being shown to be valid, the objection of *Petitio Principii* is at once turned off as applicable only to the accident of the external expression, and not to the essence of the internal thought. The analytic syllogism is not only the more natural, but is presupposed by the synthetic. It is more natural to express a reasoning in this direct and simple way than in the roundabout synthetic way.

We will next consider the most important doctrine, perhaps, which Sir William Hamilton has discovered in the domain of logic. Logicians had admitted that the *subject* of a proposition has a determinate quantity in thought, and this was accordingly expressed in language. But logicians had denied, that the *predicate* in propositions has a determinate quantity. Sir William Hamilton has, therefore, the honour to have first disclosed the principle of the thorough-going quantification of the predicate, in its full significance, in both affirmative and negative propositions. By keeping constantly in view, that logic is conversant about the internal thought, and not the external expression, he has detected more of what it is common to omit in expression, of that which is efficient in thought, than any other philosopher. Inferences, judgments, problems, are often occult in the thought, which are omitted in the expression. The purpose of common language is merely to *exhibit with clearness the matter of thought.* This is often accomplished best by omitting the expression of steps in the mental process of thinking, as the minds of others will intuitively supply the omitted steps as they follow the meaning of the elliptical expression. This elliptical character of common language has made logicians overlook the quantification of the predicate. The purpose of common language does not require the quantity to be expressed. Therefore, it was supposed that there is no quantification in the internal thought. When we reflect that all thought is a comparison of less and more, of part and whole, it is marvellous that it should not have been sooner discovered that all thought must be under some determinate quantity. And as all predication is but the expression of the internal thought, predication must have a determinate quantity—the quantity of the internal thought. But such has been the iron rule of Aristotle, that, in two thousand years, Sir William Hamilton has been the first logician who, while appreciating the labours of the Stagirite in this paramount branch of philosophy, has been in no degree enslaved by his authority, and has made improvements in and additions to logic, which almost rival those of the great founder of the science himself.

The office of logic is to exhibit *with exactness the form of thought,* and therefore to supply, in expression, the omissions of common language, whose purpose is merely to exhibit *with clearness the matter of thought.* Logic claims, therefore, as its fundamental postulate, *That we be allowed to state in language what is contained in thought.* This is exemplified in the syllogism, which is a logical statement of the form of thought in reasoning, supplying in expression what has been omitted in common language. Apply this rule to propositions, and it is at once discovered that the predicate is always of a given quantity in relation to the subject.

Upon the principle of the quantification of the predicate, Sir William Hamilton has founded an entirely new analytic of logical forms. The whole system of logic has been remodelled and simplified. The quantification of the predicate reveals, that the relation between the terms of a proposition is one not only of similarity, but of identity; and there being consequently an equation of subject and predicate, these terms are always necessarily convertible. So that simple conversion takes the place of the complex and erroneous doctrine, with its load of rules, heretofore taught by logicians.

By the new analytic, Sir William Hamilton has also amplified logic. The narrower views of logicians, in accordance with which an unnatural art had been built up, have been superseded by a wider view commensurate with nature. Logic should exhibit all the forms of thought, and not merely an arbitrary selection; and especially where they are proclaimed as all. The rules of the logicians ignore many forms of affirmation and negation, which the exigencies of thinking require, and are constantly used, but have not been noted in their abstract generality. Accordingly, Sir William Hamilton has shown that there are eight *necessary* relations of propositional terms; and, consequently, eight propositional forms performing peculiar functions in our reasonings, which are implicitly at work in our concrete thinking; and not four only, as has been generally taught. Logic has been rescued from the tedious minuteness of Aristotle, and his one-sided view, and from the trammels of technicality, and restored to the amplitude and freedom of the laws of thought.

The analysis of Sir William Hamilton enables us also to discriminate the class, and to note the differential quality of each of those syllogisms, whose forms are dependent on the internal essence of thought, and not on the contingent order of external expression, such as the disjunctive, hypothetical, and dilemmatic syllogism, and to show the special fundamental law of thought by which each distinctive reasoning is more particularly regulated. And those forms of syllogism, which are dependent on the contingent order of the external expression embraced in the three figures of Aristotle, are expounded anew; and while their legitimacy is vindicated, the fourth figure, which has been engrafted on the system by some alien hand, is shown to be a mere logical caprice. But we cannot particularize further. In fact, the workshop of the understanding has been laid open, and the materials, the moulds, and the castings of thought, in all their variety of pattern have been exhibited, and the great mystery of thinking revealed by this great master, on whom the mantle of Aristotle has fallen in the nineteenth century.

Logic may be discriminated into two grand divisions—the Doctrine of Elements, and the Doctrine of Method. Thought can only be exerted under the general laws of Identity, Contradiction, and Excluded Middle, and Reason and Consequent; and through the general forms of concepts, judgments, and reasonings. These, therefore, in their abstract generality, are the elements of thought; and that part of logic, which treats of them, is the Doctrine of Elements. To this part of logic, we have thus far confined our remarks. And the writings of Sir William Hamilton treat only of this part of logic. But, in order to show the historical position of Sir William, and to exhibit the relation which, we have said, his philosophy bears to the philosophy of Aristotle and the philosophy of Bacon, as an initial, or step of progress towards harmonizing the logic of the one with the Method of the other, it becomes necessary to remark briefly upon the second part of Logic, the Doctrine of Method.

Method is a regular procedure, governed by rules which guide us to a definite end, and guard us against aberrations. The end of Method is logical perfection, which consists in the perspicuity, the completeness, and the harmony of our knowledge. As we have shown, our knowledge supposes two conditions, one of which has relation to the thinking subject, and supposes that what is known, is known clearly, distinctly, completely, and in connection; the second has relation to what is known, and supposes that what is known, has a veritable or real existence. The former constitutes the logical, or formal perfection of knowledge; the latter, the scientific, or material perfection of knowledge. Logic, as we have shown, is conversant about the form of thought only; it is, therefore, confined exclusively to the formal perfection of our knowledge, and has nothing to do with its scientific, or material truth, or perfection. Method, therefore, consists of such rules as guide to logical perfection. These rules are, definition, division, and concatenation, or probation. The doctrine of these rules is Method.

Logic, as a system of rules, is only valuable, as a mean, towards logic as a habit of the mind—a speculative knowledge of its doctrines, and a practical dexterity with which they may be applied. Logic, therefore, both in the doctrine of elements and the doctrine of method, is discriminated into abstract or pure, and into concrete or applied. We have thus far, only had reference to abstract or pure logic; and Sir William Hamilton treats only of this. It becomes, however, necessary for our purpose, to pass into concrete or applied logic. Now, as the end of abstract, or pure logical method is merely the logical perfection of our knowledge, having reference only to the thinking subject; the end of concrete or applied logical method, is real or material truth, having reference only to the real existence of what is thought about. Concrete logic is, therefore, conversant about the laws of thought, as modified by the empirical circumstances, internal and external, in which man thinks; and, also, about the laws under which the objects of existence are to be known. We beg our readers to remember these distinctions, and that all that now follows is about concrete or applied logic.

In order to show how the improvements and developments in formal logic, which we have exhibited, that have been made by Sir William Hamilton, concilitate the deductive, or explicative logic of Aristotle, with the inductive or ampliative logic of Bacon, it becomes necessary to state the difference of the philosophical methods of the two philosophers.

The great difficulty, with the ancient philosophers of the Socratic School, was to correlate logically, the *a priori* and the *a posteriori* elements of our knowledge. The difficulty seems to have been suggested by the question, *How can we know a thing for the first time?* This question raised the doubt, that it is vain to search after a thing which we know not, since not knowing the object of our search, we should be ignorant of it when found, for we cannot recognize what we do not know. Plato, and Socrates perhaps, solved the difficulty by the doctrine, that to discover, or to learn, is but to remember what has been known by us in a prior state of existence. Investigation was thus vindicated as a valid process; and also a useful one, as it is important to recall to memory what has been forgotten. Upon this theory of knowledge, Plato made intellect, to the exclusion of sense, the faculty of scientific knowledge, and ideas or universals the sole objects of philosophical investigation. The Platonic philosophy, called, in this aspect of it, Dialectic, had for its object of investigation, the true nature of that connection which exists between each thing and the archetypal form or idea which makes it what it is, and to awaken the soul to a full remembrance of what had been known prior to being imprisoned in the body.

Aristotle made a great advance beyond Plato, towards correlating the *a priori* and *a posteriori* elements of our knowledge. He rejected the Platonic doctrine of Ideas, as universals existing anterior to and separate from singulars; and thereby ignored the Platonic doctrine of reminiscence. Still, he did not extricate himself out of the difficulties which environed the problem of human knowledge. He seems to have believed in the existence of universals or forms, not apart from, but in, particulars or singulars. And to correspond with this metaphysical doctrine, he made both intellect and sense important faculties in science. He maintained an *a priori* knowledge paramount to, but not exclusive of, the *a posteriori*. That while universals are known through the intellect, and implicitly contain particulars or singulars, yet we may be ignorant of the singulars or particulars, until realized in and through sense; and that, therefore, though all knowing is through previous knowledge, yet the investigation of particulars is not superfluous; because, while we may know the universal, we may be ignorant of the particular. Therefore, intellect and sense combine in framing the fabric of our knowledge

The Aristotelic method of investigation is, therefore, twofold, Deductive and Inductive; the first allied with intellect and with universals, the latter allied with sense and with particulars. Aristotle, in accordance with this doctrine of method, seems to have considered syllogism proper, or deduction, no less ampliative than induction—that deductive inference did, in some way, assure us, or fortify our assurance of real truth. We greatly doubt whether he discriminated at all, the difference btween formal and material inference; we think that he rather referred all difference in the cogency of inference, to the difference of necessity or contingency in the matter.* He, strangely enough, maintains for the syllogism proper, the power to deduce true conclusions from false premises. Therefore, the syllogistic inference is not wholly dependent on the premises. And consequently, Deduction is not dependent on Induction, whose office it is to supply the premises.

This logical doctrine of Aristotle corresponds with

* Kant says, "There must therefore be syllogisms which contain no empirical premises, and by means of which we conclude from something that we do know, to something of which we do not even possess a conception, to which we, nevertheless, by an unavoidable illusion, ascribe objective reality."—P. 236. Bohn.

his metaphysical, and his psychological doctrine. As he makes universals the paramount object of science, and intellect its paramount principle, so does he make syllogism the paramount process, and induction the inferior process in logic; for though intellect is not with him as with Plato, the sole principle of science, but conjunct with sense, yet sense is logically subordinate to intellect. There are, according to his theory of knowledge, certain universal principles of knowledge existing in the mind, rather as native generalities than as mere necessities of so thinking, which furnish the propositions for syllogism; therefore syllogism is not dependent for these on induction. It is nevertheless true, that according to the Aristotelic theory, there is perfect harmony between intellect and sense, between syllogism and induction. And though syllogism is the more intellectual, the more scientific; yet induction can be legitimately used as corroborative and complemental of syllogism, and particularly by weak minds, who can discern the universal in the particulars, but cannot apprehend it *a priori* as a native generality. It was because of this theory of knowledge, that induction holds so subordinate and inferior a place in the Aristotelic logic.

Whether our account of Aristotle's theory of knowledge be the true one or not, for there is much obscurity over his doctrine, it is nevertheless certain, that Aristotle had a very imperfect insight into induction as an objective process of investigation. And the slighting manner, in which he passes induction over, shows how little he appreciated it. He has made a crude and superficial distinction, which has been perpetuated to this day, between the universals derived from induction, and universals derived from similars. In other words, he has correlated induction and analogy as different kinds of reasoning. And all writers on logic, including, we suspect, even Sir William Hamilton,* still speak of reasoning by induction, and reasoning by analogy. This, it seems to us, is a great confusion and error. We make induction the process, and analogy or similarity the evidence by which the illation is warranted. That analogy, which is the mere resemblance of relations, has nothing to do with philosophy; but only that analogy, which consists of an essential resemblance or similarity. The tendency to generalize our knowledge, by the judgment, *that where partial resemblance is found, total resemblance will be found,* may be called, the principle of philosophical presumption. Upon this principle the objective process of induction is founded, by which we conclude from something observed, to something not

---

* Sir William's Class Lectures will, doubtless, give his opinions on this subject.

N.B. Since the publication of the first edition of this tract, Sir W. Hamilton's Class Lectures have been published, and, as we conjectured, he adheres to the old notion about analogy.

observed; from something within the sphere of experience, to something without its sphere. This principle of philosophical presumption, is brought to bear under two objective laws: the first proclaims, *One in many, therefore one in all;* the second proclaims, *Many in one, therefore all in one.* Through the first law, we conclude from a certain attribute being possessed by many similar things or things of the same class, that the same attribute is possessed by all similar things or things of the same class. Through the second law, we conclude from the partial similarity of two or more things in some respects, to their complete or total similarity. Both laws conclude to unity in totality; by the first, from the recognized unity in plurality; by the second, from the recognized plurality in unity. Both of the laws, it is very apparent, are phases of the principle of resemblance or analogy. To call the first of these laws *induction*, and the second, *analogy*, as has been done, destroys the correspondence between abstract or pure, and concrete or applied logic. In abstract or pure logic, induction is recognized, but analogy not; therefore analogy cannot rest on the same basis with induction in concrete or applied logic, else, like induction, it would have its counterpart in abstract logic.

The theory of knowledge, which we have expounded as his, in which the *a priori* element is so paramount to the *a posteriori*, prevented Aristotle from having any but the shallowest insight into the scope of induction. The inevitable result of this was to make him slight observation through sense; and to rely chiefly on deduction from principles supplied by the intellect. This was the cardinal vice of Plato, and also of Aristotle but not nearly to so great an extent. The philosophy, therefore, of Aristotle, is rather the result of an analysis of the contents of language, than a product of an original observation of nature. The philosophy of Bacon is just the reverse—it is a product of the observation of nature, and not an analysis of the contents of language. One of the chief precautions of the *Novum Organum* is, that language is but the registry of the crude notions of imperfect observation, and consequently that nature herself must be interpreted, to ascertain the truth. The logic of Aristotle was designed more for evolving, sifting, and methodizing what had already been thought, than for conducting new investigations. The great purpose of Bacon was to bring philosophy from books and tradition to nature, from words to things, from the Syllogism to Induction.

The true excellence of the Aristotelic logic, therefore, consists in its being considered formal and not material. In this view, the Organon of Aristotle is conversant about the laws under which the subjects thinks; while the *Novum Organum* of Bacon is conversant about the laws under which the object is to be known. Viewed in this aspect, the two logics, though contrariant, are not antagonistic; but are the complements of each other. The Aristotelic without the Baconian is null; the Baconian without the Aristotelic is deficient. The Baconian supplies the material of the Aristotelic; and while the truth of science is wholly dependent on the Baconian, its logical perfection is wholly dependent on the Aristotelic. The transition, in thinking, from the Baconian to the Aristotelic is as follows. The *process* of Induction, as founded on probability, is relative, but its conclusion is absolute. Similarities or analogies retain their character of difference and plurality in the inductive process, but become one and identical in the conclusion, or class, into which they are combined by an act of abstraction and generalization. This conclusion becomes the premise of Deduction. It is then within the domain of formal logic.

That Sir William Hamilton has done much to reconcile the Aristotelic logic with the Baconian, by purifying the theory of both, and showing their interdependence, by developing that side of the Aristotelic which lies next to particulars and induction (for all his additions to logic are such), must be admitted by those who can appreciate his writings. And nowhere, in the history of philosophy, is there a definition of Induction which reaches so thoroughly to the heart of the thing, the essential nature of the philosophical inference of the universal from the singular, as that which Sir William has given to discriminate the Baconian from the Aristotelic, the material from the formal. His definition is this: "A *material illation* of the universal from the singular, warranted either by the general analogies of nature, or by special presumptions afforded by the object-matter of any real science." This definition shows that the inductive process of Bacon is governed by the laws, not of the thinking subject, *ratione formæ*, but by the laws of the object to be known, *vi materiæ*. This definition, though only used to discriminate negatively the Aristotelic, or formal induction, sheds so much light on the Baconian induction, as to entitle Sir William Hamilton to the praise of having contributed to a true theoretic exposition of the Baconian method, by showing the ultimate basis of its validity, in disclosing the nature of the determining antecedent and the determined illation. The determining antecedent is shown to be the analogies of nature, which afford presumptions varying in all degrees of probability, from the lowest to the highest certainty, that what is found in the singulars observed is in all the singulars. The physical observer asserts, on the analogy of his science, that as *some* horned animals ruminate, *all* horned animals ruminate. The logician accepts the conclusion, all horned animals ruminate, and brings it under the laws of thought, and considers the *some* of the physical observer as equivalent to his *all*. Sir William thus extricates the theory of material induction from the syllogistic fetters in which the logicans had entangled it. His design was, however, by no means, to exalt the dominion of Bacon; but rather, all his labours are designed to draw the age from its one-sided culture—its too exclusive devotion to physics. We, therefore, standing, as we do, at the Baconian point of view of philosophy, step forward to hail the expositions of Sir William Hamilton, and concatenate them with the philosophy of Bacon. So that the Baconian philosophy, in the future, may cease to be "the dirt philosophy" which some of its heretical disciples have made it, and may embrace all the grand problems of thought which Sir William Hamilton has brought within the philosophy of common sense, and which Bacon certainly intended his philosophy to comprehend.

Having now indicated the point of conciliation, between the logics of Aristotle and of Bacon through that of Hamilton, we will suggest the course of development which the conciliated doctrine must take.

The laws of thought, in their relation to the condition of relativity, have not been expounded by Hamilton or any other philosopher. Indeed, this aspect of the laws of thought seems to have been entirely overlooked. They have been expounded only in their relation to the condition of non-contradiction. Now, in the inductive process, the condition of relativity is the one chiefly to be regarded; just as in the deductive process, that of non-contradiction is the important one.

Therefore, in giving a theoretical explication of induction, we must consider the condition of relativity. This condition, as we have shown in expounding Hamilton, is brought to bear in thinking, under two principal relations: *the relation of knowledge*, the mind thinking; and *the relation of existence*, the thing thought about. In the relation of knowledge, the mind thinking, the laws of thought are necessarily involved; because the condition of non-contradiction must be fulfilled in all thinking. In fact, the conditions of non-contradiction and relativity are mutually dependent and reciprocally relative. But hitherto, the relation of existence, the thing thought about, has been considered, in explaining the inductive process, to the total neglect of the relation of the mind thinking. The objective element of thought has been considered to the exclusion of the subjective element. The objective, it is true, is the great determining element in induction, and therefore, the more obtrusive and important, and very properly and naturally first attracted reflective attention. But then, in giving a theoretical explication of induction, it is indispensable that the subjective element of thought be regarded. In this aspect of the problem of induction, the condition of non-contradiction in its three-fold application under the laws of identity, contradiction and excluded middle, must be expounded.

In the future, therefore, the chief point of development, in applied logic, will consist in showing the empirical application of the laws of thought in the inductive process. Principles, which have hitherto been considered primary regulatives, will be resolved into intermediate axioms, mere special applications of the law of identity through the principle of philosophical presumption. All actual, positive thinking is, the identification of the plural under the conditions of non-contradiction and relativity. In the deductive process, which is especially dependent on the condition of non-contradiction, total identity is the objective law; and therefore, the process is only explicative. But in the inductive process, which is especially dependent on the condition of relativity, the one prime law of the objective on which the process is dependent, is analogy or partial identity; therefore, the process is ampliative, because the partial identity is shown in the totalizing result to be total identity when extricated from the diversity which modified it into apparently partial identity. The field of identity is thereby enlarged, and that of diversity lessened—knowledge is increased and ignorance diminished. The judgment, therefore, called *the principle of philosophical presumption*, that where partial resemblance (partial identity) is found, total resemblance (total identity) will be found, is thus shown to be under the immediate guidance of the law of identity in its empirical application. Hence, the principle of philosophical presumption determined by the objective law of analogy, correlated with the laws of thought, constitute the basis of a valid theoretical exposition of induction. And the details of a practical system will consist of the rules of all special judgments determined by the special object matters or analogies.

The logic of inference has, therefore, for its object matter, the laws of thought in their empirical application. In developing this logic, truths which have hitherto been considered necessary, will be found to be only experiential axioms applied in actual thinking under the guidance of the laws of thought. Our original and our acquired perceptions, and our necessary and our experiential notions are so interdependent in our mental operations, that reflective analysis has as yet failed to sufficiently separate them in thought. *A priori* principles are only discovered *a posteriori.* Consciousness is only cognizant of the individual act, and has not before it the *a priori* principle or regulative which is found by reflective analysis to be the pole on which the thinking turned. This is the case of *the principle of the uniformity of nature.* This principle, as a known truth, is only an empirical generalization. The law of identity conducts thinking to the same affirmatives without any reference either implicit or explicit to any such principle. The uniformity of nature is an after reflection. It is not even an assumption, except in the descending scale or process of induction. The principle of philosophical presumption is therefore not prompted by the assumption of the uniformity of nature, but is under the guidance of the law of identity, and is but a modification of the mental tendency to bring multiplicity to unity.

As a preparative to this completer logic of inference, criticism must ascertain, distinguish, and correlate, the primary beliefs with the several cognitive faculties and with the laws of thought in their empirical application. The primary beliefs are not near so numerous, as the spirit of the Scotch philosophy and its uncritical state in this respect, seem to show.

We will now indicate what, we think, should be the future course of metaphysics.

The criticism by Sir William Hamilton, which we have exhibited, has established, that we can *know* nothing beyond the limitation of consciousness. Any existence, therefore, beyond this limitation, can only be an object of faith. Metaphysics which is the science of that which transcends knowledge must rest upon faith. But then, has not faith its limits? If it has none, then it is as legitimate to believe one thing as another, which is equivalent to having no faith. Therefore the principle of contradiction, which is a limit to the possible in existence as well as in thought, constrains us to set a limit to faith. This limit is, the condition of relativity, which is the condition of consciousness. We can only believe in the absolute or infinite through the relative and the finite. We can believe in nothing which has not its germ in some one or more presentations of consciousness. We therefore, entirely repudiate all that wild faith which is divorced from the understanding. No faith is valid whose object, the laws of the understanding do not constrain us to infer, from data of consciousness, as existent. To posit in existence any object which the understanding does not place there, by the constraint of its laws exercised upon the data of consciousness, is pure conjecture. The laws of the understanding, as we have shown, are regulatives to all inferences as well as to all deductions. To let faith go in a direction which they do not indicate, is to revolt against reason as limited in man. Sir William Hamilton was right, therefore, in seeking for a logical basis for his metaphysics; though, perhaps, he did not see the full import of the doctrine. He found this basis in the logico-metaphysical principle of two contradictory extremes conditioning thought. And by applying the law of excluded middle, he does not, as some have supposed, get a mere formal conclusion; because the laws of thought, as we have shown, are applicable to inference or material conclusion. Nor does he thereby surreptitiously introduce, as has been said, what he has explicitly rejected; for he does not, thereby, make the absolute or infinite an object of knowledge, but only of faith.

All metaphysical inquiry is, therefore, confined to

the question, What does the logical understanding constrain or authorize us to believe in regard to the transcendental? It constrains us: 1. To believe that time and space are infinite. Because we contradict ourselves, in attempting to think that either is not infinite. This settled: 2. We are further constrained to think, that infinite substantive existence *is possible*. Because, time and space are the infinite conditions of substantive existence, being in themselves of such a nature as neither to exclude each other, nor to constitute being in such a mode as to exclude other existences. They are in fact, in their relation to substantive existence, purely negative. Here the question emerges, What existence does the logical understanding, exercised upon the data of consciousness, constrain us to project into the unoccupied conditions of time and space? It certainly does not necessitate us to fill them with infinite worlds or with a supersensible world. It does, however, constrain us to project an absolute cause; for in thinking about causation as given in consciousness, we contradict ourselves by attempting to think it as absolutely beginning. And the judging faculty, from which all the interpreting light must come, realizes, that its thinking about finite things is not logically complete unless an absolute cause be posited in existence. An infinite series of causes, the other alternative, does not satisfy the understanding; because it recedes in endless negation. Metaphysics therefore culminates in theology.

God is the ultimate problem to which all the lines of philosophical investigation conduct. It is, therefore, proper for philosophy to inquire, whether, from a speculative point of view, Christianity is entitled to the high pretensions which it assumes, of being a revelation from God of transcendental truths pertaining to the respective characters of God and man, and from these characters explaining the government of the one, and disclosing the duties of the other.

It is obvious that if philosophy must, from the principles and the laws of human reason, pronounce, there is no God; or if it must pronounce, from these principles and these laws, that man has no right of intelligence either to believe or disbelieve in a God, Christianity must, rationally, fall under the same adverse judgment. But if, on the other hand, it can be shown that, speculatively, atheism is impossible, and the understanding is thereby remitted to the evidences of natural theology, untrammelled by any *a priori* or speculative doubt, and that the great fact which Christianity assumes, that there is a God, stands on the rational ground of a conviction constrained by the most insuperable negative considerations, and by the most diverse positive evidence, Christianity thus becomes possible as a divine revelation, and is remitted to its proper evidences for proof of its high pretension.

It thus becomes manifest that the first requirement

of a speculative proof of Christianity is, to show that there is a God to make such a revelation And if the philosophical proof of a God shall disclose him to human understanding, under the same special representations in which he is revealed in Christianity, this will be a cogent reason for the truth of Christianity. For if the most scientific thought will disclose an inference so complex in its premises in regard to the most difficult of questions, in just the same form and limits in which it is presented in a doctrine taught by unscientific thinkers, who profess that the doctrine was received from a higher intelligence than their own, or if the author, though illiterate, professes to be a higher intelligence than man, it is evidence of both the authority and truth of the doctrine. Christianity attempts no proof of the existence of a God ; and, therefore, it only speaks of him, as if his existence were admitted. Christ came not as a philosopher, with reasons to authenticate his mission and his doctrine, but as more than a philosopher, with miracles suspending the laws of nature which philosophers can only learn so far as to obey them.

Criticisms of theology, both natural and revealed, correspond with the respective schemes of philosophy of which they are the polemic applications. Sensualism and Intellectualism, the philosophical opposites of each other, put forth their respective principles as tests by which the problem of God is to be solved, and also by which Christianity is to be criticised. The first, at most, makes God a law or force; and the last strips him of all personality and all relations, and presents him in the nakedness and solitude of metaphysical abstraction—a mere pantheistic self-contradiction—a nothing. The first, as in the doctrine of Paulus, converts, by a sensualistic interpretation, the supernatural facts of Christianity into ordinary physical phenomena, misunderstood by an easy credulity. The glory of our Lord, which, on the night of his birth, shone around the shepherds of Jerusalem, was, according to Paulus, an *ignis fatuus*, or meteor; and the ascension of the Lord was nothing more than his sudden disappearance behind a cloud that accidentally intervened between him and his disciples. The last, as in the doctrine of Straus, by a pantheistic interpretation, converts Christianity into a myth, a poetical fiction, representing religious ideas in the form of facts which were believed by the authors of the Gospels to have actually occurred. The ideas symbolized in the facts of the evangelical myths are, according to Straus, true as applied to humanity as a whole, but false as applied to the individual. But in the one-sided theories of the human mind, of Sensualism and Intellectualism, man's reason is put at war with itself. Both are true as a principle, but false as a theory. When Epicurus asserted that reality resides in senuous objects alone, and that all else is imaginary; and when Plato proclaimed, that the senses are only sources of illusion, and that all reality is in intelligible objects which can be seen only by an intuition apart from sense, two theories hostile in their scopes and aims were ushered upon the battle-field of speculation, which have never yet come to terms of entire reconciliation. But as each theory is only a perverted truth, by which a part is substituted for the whole, each having a principle in the human mind for its basis, philosophers have endeavoured to reconcile the two principles in theories of mind embracing both. The most remarkable of these is Kant's Critique of Pure Reason. By a too architectural view of the human intelligence, Kant has so exhibited the human mind, as to make the principle on which Sensualism reposes a mere receptivity of illusions circumscribed and conditioned by conceptions that are also illusions; and the principle on which Intellectualism reposes, he makes an illusive regulator of the other illusions. So that Kant has reconciled the antecedent hostile theories of Sensualism and Intellectualism, not by showing that there is no real hostility between the faculties of the human mind, when both principles on which they respectively repose are recognized, but by making human intelligence utterly mendacious. And worse than this, he makes the lower faculty find its highest function in striving to realize, as objectively true, the impossible illusions which are shadowed forth by the highest faculty, and which, though illusive, all the aspirations of man's intellectual and moral natures make him hope and believe to be true.

It is upon this false theory of human intelligence that Kant has built the most potent and subtle polemic against the speculative validity of theism, as a rational doctrine, which has ever been taught. But the force of his criticism depends, for the most part, upon the chasm which he erroneously represents as existing between the lower and the higher faculties of human intelligence, in the normal exercise of their respective functions; so that the higher, which is above all possible experience, can never derive any light from experience in proof of its ideas as having corresponding objects in being, but must ever wander, lost in the midst of paradoxes which it is constrained to own as the legitimate products of its function, and which, at best, can only be systematized into insoluble antinomies or necessary conflicts of reason. On this scheme of human intelligence it is that Kant starts on the examination of the proofs of the existence of a supreme being, assuming, as his theory of the mind compelled him to do, that the notion of God is a mere necessary idea of the highest faculty of man, the objective validity of which it is impossible either to prove or disprove. However the aspirations of the human heart may offer up the incense of contrition and worship, after all, according to Kant, the object of adoration is, to speculative reason, only an idea hypostatized and personified by empirical credulity. What is worshipped as God is a mere regulative idea, to give scientific unity to the illusions of sense, its value being logical, not moral, scientific, not theological. But yet, as speculation cannot, according to Kant, either affirm or deny the existence of a supreme being, it relegates the question to empirical proofs which may elicit a belief, but not a cognition, for the idea lies out of the field of possible experience. Such is the rationale of Kant's transcendental criticism of theology or the problem of God. And though he relegates the problem to empirical proofs, upon his scheme of the faculties of human thought, these proofs have no real validity. For, while he states the empirical or physico-theological proofs with great force of logical combination, they are eviscerated of their cogency because of the entire separation, in his theory of human intelligence, of the sensuous intuition and its contents from pure reason and its ideas, of which God is one. Kant's theory of the human intelligence is so revolting to common sense that even his own perverse ingenuity at times seems to be on the eve of discerning its sophistical character. In the following sentence he comes near to surrendering it as a blunder: "The reason (says Kant) does not properly give birth to any conception, but only frees the conception from the unavoidable limitation of a possible experience; and thus endeavours to raise it above the empirical, though it must still be *in connection* with it. Transcendental ideas are properly nothing but categories elevated to the unconditioned." Our highest thought, as this sentence nearly expresses, is a continuous thread, beginning in the intuitions of the external and internal senses, and is woven exclusively of the elements furnished by these primary faculties. There is no contribution of material by any higher faculty. There is a transcendental element in the primary intuitions—in experience—by which the mind rises necessarily toward the unconditioned, not as something *known*, but believed; being relatively implied in that which is known. This transcendental element is the relation in human thought of the conceivable to the inconceivable. For the conceivable in human knowledge is always bounded by the inconceivable, being always conceived in relation to it; and the mind, by a logical necessity, as well as by an intelligent craving, ever strives to comprehend the inconceivable or unconditioned. Therefore, though in human thinking the conceivable and the inconceivable are, logically, mutually exclusive of each other, yet, psychologically, they are mutually relative and intelligently filiated, and together make up that quantum of human knowledge and belief which, according to the laws of intelligence, must have objective validity. This truth is realized in the fact, that it is impossible to conceive either an absolute least or an absolute greatest. There is always something beyond, which, though inconceivable, is necessarily believed to exist. Knowledge is, therefore, bounded by faith. Kant extinguished by his theory the transcendental ray in experience, and made the whole region beyond actual knowledge one of outer darkness. In his view of experience, speculation must ignore a God. But in our view of experience, the transcendental element or relation is a clew to conduct us through the labyrinth of negations, which meet us on all sides with their contradiction, to the goal where reason is necessitated by its own laws, as will presently be shown, to believe in a God, or else ignore its primary beliefs and nullify its rationality. And the argument founded on merely rational principles is supplemented and corroborated by the sense of moral obligation and the profound moral interests which a spirit, like man's, feels in the destiny which is foreshadowed by the reckonings of his reason. For our spiritual instincts are deliverences of intelligence, and have their proper objects of fruition in the universe.

Having exposed the sophistry of the objections offered by the Kantean philosophy against the validity of the argument for a God, we will proceed to examine the problem of God as it rests upon its intrinsic evidences. The clew to the solution of the problem is to be found in the doctrine of causation. The notion of cause is the clew by which the phenomena of the physical world are unravelled. Physical science does not transcend the horizon of natural causes, which are conceived as blindly operating forces inherent in matter. But as no natural cause is conceived as self-sufficient, but must be considered only as an effect of a cause, and thus, in an endless regress into infinity, the science of metaphysics emerges in human thinking, as an explanation of what lies beyond the horizon of natural causes. Two theories, to which all others may be reduced, after eliminating the irrelevant modifications, are given of the metaphysical notion of a cause. The one is that the notion is the result of an impotence to think an absolute beginning, and therefore is purely negative, importing only a limitation of knowledge. The other and older and most generally received theory is, that the notion is the product of the consciousness of the exercise of force by our will upon our physical organization, and that this notion is transferred to all the changes in the physical world, as representative of their antecedent; the notion of cause being connected with the observed change, either by a law of association, according to some, or by a necessary law of thought, according to others. But neither the positive nor the negative theory is self-sufficient. Neither is an adequate explanation of the contingent in nature; and more especially does neither explain how effects or changes result in arrangements indicating design or final purpose. These arrangements, called final causes, are the one obtrusive manifestation characterizing universal nature; and the arrangements are not only perfect in mechanical skill and calculated with the nicest mathematical accuracy in weight and measure and forces, but the artistic finish and ornament is consummate in skill and beauty, each having no relation to a blind force, nor to any conceivable antecedent, except an intelligent creator of surpassing knowledge, taste, and power. And as an antecedent is necessarily thought, on either theory of causation, atheism, or disbelief in the existence of an intelligent artificer adequate to such work, is both a scientific and metaphysical impossibility. To suppose that the whole work is self-originated, is to ignore all intelligence, and thus to ignore the supposition itself, which is self-contradictory. Causation, in ultimate analysis, must be conceived as that which is self-determined; and when it is ascribed to physical nature, the inference is according to the analogy of man, and not according to the analogy of the world or physical nature; for cause must be conceived as originating in, if not identical with, intelligence and will. It is by this sort of inference that we determine the character or nature of our fellow-men. It is through our own image that we behold them. We are, by the laws of thought, necessitated to transfer to them our own forms of thought and our entire personality. By this same necessity, we are constrained to infer, from the data of self-consciousness, in connection with causation in the physical world, that God is; and that he is a person, a conscious intelligence like ourselves, and not a mere law or force. We cannot stop short at a mere *deus ex machina*, which physical nature with its forces indicates as its fabricator, but we are constrained to add, to God's nature, those attributes which are indicated in the providences shown in the bounties of physical nature, with its rotation of seasons and their respective beneficences; and also those moral attributes which are indicated in the sublime mystery of human conscience determining right and wrong, sin and righteous condemnation; and which utters its voice with undiminished authority, even when man is conscious that a passion binds him as inexorably as fate, and, that, while he feels that his only hope is heaven and his only help is prayer, yet his sin stifles his prayer and his hope, and makes him curse God, while he feels that God is long-suffering and slow to anger.

Feeling, and belief, and knowledge are distinguishable, but yet essentially and inseparably connected, elements of our intelligent nature. Therefore, in considering the grounds and proofs of God, we must estimate the force of each of these elements, in determining the existence and the character of God, as manifested in his relations to man and the world. We must not eliminate feeling and sentiment, and other anthropomorphic elements from ratiocination, as we do, in a mere inductive process of scientific inquiry, when seeking for an ultimate ground of science, where we must, as Bacon says, not draw our inferences *ex analogia hominis*, but *ex analogia universi*. But in the inquiry for a God, the inferences are legitimately *ex analogia hominis*, though founded on manifestations in the physical world. "Though man be not identical with the deity," says Hamilton, "still, he is created in the image of God. It is indeed only through analogy of the human with the divine, that we are percipient and recipient of the divinity." The personifying propensity, which induces man to personify external physical objects, must be taken into consideration in the evidences for a God; as it is a normal function of the mind, and indispensable to make up the complement of human faculties necessary to acquire the truths which pertain to human knowledge and human happiness. The Greeks personified the physical forces, and supposed that the course of nature was carried on by direct supernatural personal agency. And when Socrates taught the doctrine of second causes, Aristophanes ridiculed the doctrine, in the comedy of "The Clouds," as blasphemous and atheistic, thereby showing the common opinion of the Greeks. It is by this function of the human mind that the personality of God is determined.

The logical cogency of the foregoing argument can be estimated, and its apodictic certainty demonstrated, by reference to the laws of thought by which the process is necessitated. For the synthetic and ampliative process of reason, by which inference from the data of consciousness is made upon analogy, is, logically, as cogent as the analytic and explicative process of reason, by which deduction is made from premises. The only difference is, that the mind is more liable to error by paralogism in the ampliative process than in the explicative; because, in the ampliative process, analogy has to be estimated, and may be misunderstood. But if the analogy be a valid one, the conclusion is determined with absolute certainty. For though logicians have not discovered that the ampliative process, as well as the explicative, is under the necessary laws of thought, analysis can demonstrate the fact Because analogy, on which the ampliative process is founded, is only identity or sameness involved in diversity; and the ampliative process disentangles it from the diversity, and unifies it, by the law of identity, with the data of consciousness which suggested the analogy. Therefore, from the notions of personality, and of intelligence and will, and of cause and design, given in human consciousness, we are constrained, by the law of identity, to affirm, from the indications of the physical world, that a personal intelligence, with a will and power like our own, has fabricated it, and exists as its governor.

To deny this, is to deny what the law of identity constrains us to affirm, and therefore is self-contradictory. If the analogy be not mistaken, the inference is necessitated. And it is equally self-contradictory to deny the analogy.

The argument for a God, therefore, when tested by logical analysis, if we admit, as we are bound to do, the supreme authority of the necessary laws of thought over the field of speculation, is found to be apodictically certain. God belongs to that class of truths which the laws of the understanding constrain us to believe, from the data derived from internal and external observation. It was by the laws of the understanding that Leverier was constrained to believe, from the data of observation, the existence of the planet Neptune, which afterwards became an object of intuition through the telescope. God, though believed in, by a like process of conviction, cannot become an object of direct knowledge, as will be explained in the sequel.

Admit, therefore, the reality of the external world, with its evidences of design, and atheism is speculatively impossible. Is then the sensible universe a mere illusion? This is a fitting inquiry for one who can say in his heart, There is no God. It is proper to show such an one, that the magnificent spectacle of order, beauty, and conformity to ends, called the world, as well as the grand glories, called the heavens, are not illusions of his own faculty, which he calls reason.

The universal doctrine of the ancient philosophy was adverse to natural realism, maintaining as it did, that we cannot perceive the external world immediately, but only by means of ideas; and therefore the ancient doctrine is called idealism. The philosophy of Bacon was a recoil against idealism. Observation of the external world, upon trust in the senses, was the one great precept of his philosophy—assuming that the external world is distinct from the mind, and is real; its whole aim is natural realism. Locke, in continuing the Baconian movement, inconsistently fell into the common error, traditionally received from the ancient philosophy, that we do not immediately perceive the external world, but something representative of it. By thus encumbering observation with a false hypothesis, repugnant to the validity of observation, Locke's philosophy was pregnant with covert absurdity. Therefore it was, that Hume, in the spirit of skepticism, accepted the doctrine of Locke, and exposed the absurdity which it involved. Hume, in fact, showed that philosophy is either altogether a delusion, or that the doctrine of Locke is erroneous or incomplete. Hume's doctrine was a scientific and technical ignorance, aiming at the overthrow, especially, of a God as a valid philosophical belief. Philosophers were, therefore, constrained either to surrender philosophy as impossible, or else to ascend to higher principles for defence against skeptical reduction. Hume thus put philosophy into a dilemma, that forms a memorable crisis in the history of speculation.

His Skepticism awoke the Sensualism of Britain, and the Intellectualism of Germany, from their respective dogmatic slumber, reposing, as each did, upon its own special principle, without any due acknowledgment of that of the other. It was manifest that the problems of philosophy must be considered in new aspects, and be subjected to a more searching analysis. As speculation had done, in all periods before, it took two opposite courses: British philosophy took the course which trusts more to the senses, and German philosophy took the course which relies more upon the ability of the intellect; hence we have designated the first Sensualism, and the last Intellectualism.

Reid, it was, who attempted to rescue British philosophy from the skepticism of Hume. He saw that Hume's reasoning proved, that the doctrine of representative perception involved, not only the denial of the existence of matter, but, by the fairest sequence, the denial of the substantiality of mind. He, therefore, strove to vindicate the unconditional veracity of consciousness, which testifies that we do immediately perceive the external world; and, by analysis of mental phenomena, he established the cardinal doctrine in metaphysics, *That what our nature compels us to believe as true and real, is true and real*, called the doctrine of common sense.

Kant, startled, like Reid, by the skepticism of Hume, strove to connect cause and effect, which Hume had shown, upon the doctrine of Sensualism, to be correlated only by succession in nature and by custom in thought. Kant makes causation the central problem of his philosophy, in accordance with his Intellectualism, which makes the notion of cause a mere regulative idea or logical principle unifying, into a scientific whole, the contents of sensuous intuition, and having no objective validity; while Reid made external perception the central problem of his philosophy, in accordance with Sensualism which reposes confidence in the senses as the accredited messengers of consciousness. But Kant decided the adverse destiny of his philosophy by his first step: He clung to the old idealism, that we do not immediately perceive external objects: but that what we illusively see, as the external world, is only a modification of our minds, and reality is only a necessary illusion. Having thus declared consciousness untrustworthy, his philosophy ended in making human intelligence self-contradictory in its normal exercise. And as, according to his philosophy, truth consists in the harmony of thought with thought, and not of thought with things, the spirit of his philosophy encouraged the most unexclusive doubt.

The doctrine of Kant, that the external world is a necessary illusion imposed on us by a treacherous reason, admitted, however, that there may be a reality corresponding to the necessary illusion. In this aspect, his philosophy is a hypothetical realism. But Fichte showed, by a rigorous logical analysis, that, at bottom, Kant's philosophy is absolute idealism denying any external world. Kant expressly taught, in accordance with the spirit of his philosophy, as we have seen, that the notion of God is only an idea with no objective validity possible to human reason.

The problem of reality and God, being thus decided in the negative by Kant, who had opened up the way of Intellectualism in refutation of Hume's skepticism, Schelling, proceeding in the same direction with Kant, claimed, for the mind of man, what Kant had demonstrated to be impossible, a faculty of intellectual intuition which is apart from sense, above consciousness, and released from the laws of the understanding, and which comprehends the absolute by becoming the absolute, and thus knows God by being God. By thus cutting the Gordean knot of metaphysics, Schelling thought that he had explained the knowledge of external reality and of God.

Hegel, the disciple of Schelling, next attempted to solve the problem of existence and of knowledge: and while ridiculing the intellectual intuition of his master as a poetical play of fancy, he claimed, that by sifting mental phenomena, men can rise to absolute knowledge, through a dialectical process which starts from the thesis, that being and nothing are the same; and that so far is contradiction, from being an insuperable barrier to intellectual cognition, it is the chief instrument in laying the foundation of our higher knowledge, which, in fact, ends in the consummate paradox and ultimate truth, that contradictories are one and universal negativity is the essence of thought. And Oken, another disciple of Schelling, only a little less distinguished than Hegel, in the true spirit and principle of this philosophy, proclaimed, that God is nothing, and nothing is God; so impossible is it for human reason to deny the existence of God, that a philosophy, which outrages the conditions of thought and ends in universal negation, makes that negation God.

It was in this state of the problem of realism, that Sir William Hamilton took up the subject. He showed the intellectual realism of Schelling and his school to be a scheme of mere negation. And he proclaimed, in its stead, the doctrine of natural realism. "A mental operation (says Hamilton) is only what it is by relation to its object; the object at once determining its existence and specifying the character of its existence." This restoration of the objective to its legitimate position, in the dualism of thought and existence, from which Kant had displaced it, Hamilton based upon Reid's doctrine of common sense. Natural realism, while it recognizes the relativity of thought, excludes that void relativity of Kant which makes philosophy a scheme of mere formal relations, just as entirely as it excludes the intellectual realism of Schelling and his school, which identifies the objective and the subjective in a unitarianism of thought and existence.

We are therefore remitted, by all the efforts of speculation to solve the problem of knowledge and existence, to the doctrine of natural realism, that there is a real external world, which we know immediately, reposing upon the principle, that what our nature constrains us to believe as true and real, is true and real. And all, or nearly all the intellectualists, after the self-love, which, in speculation, is apt to overcome the love of truth, had abated, have abandoned their ambitious doctrine of omniscience, and acknowledged the catholic confession of philosophy proposed by Bacon, that in order to enter the temple of science, we must become as little children, trusting to necessary beliefs. In this spirit we have examined the problem of God; and have, we submit, contrary to the doctrine of Kant, that theism is speculatively impossible, shown that atheism is not only speculatively impossible, but that we are, upon the empirical proofs, necessitated by the laws of thought to believe in a God.

But, though we have shown that we must believe in a personal God, of intelligence, will, and moral nature like our own, the question arises, is he omniscient, omnipotent, and morally perfect? as the proclivities of the human mind certainly urge men to assert. We cannot *know* that God is omniscient, or omnipotent, or morally perfect; for we have not, in our natures, any cognitive measure of these unlimited attributes. We can at most, therefore, only infer and believe that God possesses these transcendental attributes.

There is, however, as we have already shown, a philosophy which aspires to know God absolutely. That philosophy has proposed two modes for this knowledge. Schelling proposes an intellectual intuition free from all the conditions of sensuous intuition; and Hegel proposes a dialectical process free from the laws of thought. So unsatisfactory was the mode of each to the other, that while Hegel, as we have already said, calls the intellectual intuition a poetical play of fancy, Schelling calls the dialectical process a logical play with words. In fact, both modes of knowing are so absurd, ignoring, as each does, all the limitations of the human understanding, that it would have been a marvel in human error, if two such great thinkers had agreed in either mode. Each mode involves the doctrine of intellectual realism, and consummates its irrationality, as we have shown, in making God nothing, and nothing God. For, in fact, the absolute and infinite of this philosophy are subjective negations commuted into objective affirmations. But as thoroughly as all this has been exposed by Sir William Hamilton, there are respectable writers on metaphysics who still assert that man can know the infinite. Therefore it is, that we yield to the necessity of briefly considering the question.

If by knowledge we mean the immediate cognition of an object, then we can only know God by the intellectual intuition of Schelling. If we enlarge the notion of knowledge, so as to embrace whatever can be evolved in a dialectical process, then we must have the dialectic of Hegel to know God. There is no other method of knowing God even conceivable by the most perverse ingenuity. To know God, therefore, we must follow either Schelling or Hegel. But if we admit, as we must, that consciousness is the prime condition of human intelligence, how can we cognize the infinite or absolute, when the fundamental law of consciousness is an antithesis of a subject thinking an object? Therefore, in the peculiar meaning of the philosophy of Schelling and Hegel, the subject has to become the infinite or absolute object in order to know it; for otherwise the subject would not be embraced in the absolute or all (the absolute and infinite mean the all, in this philosophy), which would be a contradiction.

The words *absolute* and *infinite* express the inconceivable in two counter forms. The word *inconceivable* has a valid meaning, though it does not involve the conception of the object which it denotes, but negatives the possibility of such a conception. All negation involves affirmation, and we cannot predicate non-existence except by reference to existence; therefore, when we predicate infiniteness or inconceivability, it is always by reference to some finite or conceivable thing. Negative thinking is realized only under the condition of relativity and positive thinking. It expresses the limitation and impotency of the human understanding in a form that indicates an attempt and failure to conceive; and though it is objective in expression, and denotes negation, yet the negation implies subjective impotency and not objective impossibility. Room is therefore left for belief of the objective possibility of that which, in our failure to conceive it, we call the infinite. Knowledge is, therefore, not the whole contents of human intelligence; but faith is given to supplement, by its less certain, but not less valid conviction, the impotency of reason or understanding. The conception, called the infinite, is generated in an attempt to separate the conditions of finiteness—of relativity and non-contradiction—from a given object, that is, to conceive it absolutely; and the conscious failure leads to calling the object infinite or unfinishable in thought; and all that the conception embraces, in our attempt to think, from the finite to the absolute, is the indefinite, which we call the infinite. This psychological genesis of the notion of the infinite, shows that belief in the infinite is not a mere instinct or feeling, but a necessitated conviction inseparably incident to the impotency of the understanding, being only a less certain conviction of reason

Though, therefore, the absolute nature of God is not directly manifested, and cannot be, to the reason of man, yet he is manifested under finite symbols and relations, which have a positive significance, and indicate, indirectly, that God is greater than the finite meaning of the symbols and relations; and the laws of our intelligence constrain us to believe, from what we know of him in his relations, in his incomprehensible majesty. In fact, we *know* that God is incomprehensible; for our consciousness testifies that nescience exercises an important function in our intelligent convictions in regard to the nature of God. This nescience of God is not atheism, but just the reverse; while the doctrine of absolute knowledge of God is atheism; for the philosophical conception, in which that pretended knowledge consists, is a mere negation, as we have shown. Though, therefore, final causes, together with our own personality, do not reveal the fulness of the Godhead to us, we are not on that account atheists, but theists, knowing in part, and believing more than we know; and hoping for the time when we shall know even as we are known.

There is no medium between apprehending an infinite being directly and analogically. That such being cannot be apprehended directly, we have shown. And that analogy debars absolute knowledge, is manifest. But so it be admitted, as it must, that all our intelligence of God is by analogy, it matters but little, practically, whether the mental conviction be called knowledge, belief, or faith.

Having, as we trust, shown that we are constrained, by the laws of thought, to believe, from the data of consciousness, in a personal God, who is incomprehensible; and thereby, having also established the doctrine, that we are compelled, by our intelligent nature, to believe a thing, though we may not be able to comprehend it, we are prepared to enter upon considerations which will conduct us to a position, from which we can take a speculative view of Christianity, as a supernatural revelation, from the God whose existence we have proved.

That man is a moral, and therefore accountable agent, and yet hemmed in by insurmountable impediments to free action, has always been more or less obvious to the common sense and the speculative reason of man. Hence human life has always been, to the mind of man, an insoluble paradox. The physical world so manifestly presents irresistible and irreversible courses of events, that their necessity, against all human power, has never been doubted. And when the courses of the moral world are scanned, the human mind is necessitated, by the laws of its intelligence, to predicate causation between the antecedents and consequents; and has never been able to construe, to consciousness, the difference between the forces of nature and the motives of a rational will, in determining necessary results, though they must be, and are, assumed as different in our practical convictions. So that, to the ancient Greek popular mind, both the physical and moral worlds seemed equally bound in fate. And yet sin seemed, to the pagan mind, a prime fact in the world, and punishment an inevitable retribution. It seemed to the Greeks as if there was an alliance and compact between the fates or powers of nature, and the furies or powers of conscience, to punish man for acts to which he is inexorably doomed, and for which, nevertheless, he could not but feel he was morally responsible. This terrible doctrine or belief, appears, in all its import, in the Greek drama, that living picture of Greek life. An inexorable fate seems to rule all the actions of the drama, to an inevitable destiny. Clytemnestra, who appears in so many dramas, by different poets, and is therefore a good example of the Greek conscience, does not, in her moral agonies, so much feel the remorse which results from conscious guilt, as the cruel torture of an inexorable fate. Though she had participated in the murder of her husband, the guilt of so foul a deed sat light upon her heart, even after she had reflected upon its turpitude; but she dreaded the furies as the scourges of fate. In Greek life, the pagan or heathen conscience attained its highest enlightenment; and the actors in the Greek drama reveal, in a striking manner, the various workings of the pagan conscience.

And the doctrines of the Greek philosophers, Plato and Aristotle, in regard to the great facts of the moral world, were but little, if at all, more satisfactory than the common opinions of the people. These philosophers taught that matter is eternal, and that evil in the world is owing to the want of its perfect adaptability to good. Nature, they taught, always tends in its operations towards good, but owing to the imperfection of matter, which refuses to adjust itself to the form, it does not always, in its formations, attain to good. The soul, they taught, is the end and the essence of the body in all animals. In the souls of the inferior animals, the end of nature is not perfectly accomplished; neither is it in the souls of children. The human animal, and that the male, is the end and the centre of all earthly natures. All else beneath the moon is, as it were, an unsuccessful attempt to produce the male man.

Aristotle looked upon the reason of man as an element emigrated, from another sphere, into this sublunary portion of the universe. The moral life of man, therefore, he considered as an interpolation in nature—something distinct from the rest of the world. The end of his ethics is, to determine what is good for man politically, socially, and individually, in this life. Morality, in his system, is a relative mean between the opposite vices of excess and deficiency; and the rule of right is to be determined by the majority of instances. Virtue is a disposition towards good acquired by habit. Men who live rationally are, he thought, especially dear to the gods, and the peculiar objects of their providence; but that external and corporeal advantages are rather things of fortune, which, as they do not always fall to the share of the good and deserving, it is hard to say whether they are dispensed by the gods or not. Socrates maintained, and so did Plato, but not so exclusively, that virtue follows from knowledge, and that man only transgresses involuntarily.

The Greek mind, representing, as it did, the highest pagan or heathen enlightenment, was wholly unable to reconcile the moral phenomena of the course of natural providence with the judgments of their moral sense. The adversity of the good, the prosperity of the wicked, the crimes of the guilty involving the misery of the innocent, and even the existence of evil at all, whether physical or moral, perplexed their reason with insoluble paradoxes. The Greeks, amongst other opinions in regard to the moral administration of the world, believed that Jupiter kept his lightnings to punish perjury; for physical punishment, because of moral delinquency, was a cardinal notion of the Greeks in regard to the course of nature. Aristophanes, in the comedy of "The Clouds," exposes the paradox which the belief involves; and thereby illustrates the moral preplexities which environed Greek opinion of the providential course of nature. Aristophanes is ridiculing the doctrine of second causes, as taking the administration of the world out of the hands of the gods, and presents Socrates as teaching the doctrine to Strepsiades, who held on to the popular opinion of the agency of the gods.

"*Strep.* Let that pass,
And tell me of the lightning, whose quick flash
Burns us to cinders; that, at least, great Jove
Keeps in reserve to launch at perjury?
*Socr.* Dunce, dotard! were you born before the flood,
To talk of perjury, whilst Simon breathes,
Theorus and Cleonymus; whilst they,
Thrice-perjured villains, brave the lightning's stroke,
And gaze the heav'ns unscorcht? Would these escape?
Why, man, Jove's random fires strike his own fane,
Strike Sunium's guiltless top, strike the dumb oak,
Who never yet broke faith, or falsely swore."

The perennial fact, in human judgment, that God's moral administration of this world has always seemed, to human reason, less perfect in justice than the moral standard which man sets up, in each age, as the criterion of moral conduct, seems conclusive, that the finite moral conceptions of man furnish no adequate type of the rule of God's conduct, whose ways are not as our ways, in his eternal administration over the life of man. And as man cannot obtain a conception of the infinite character of God, the Greeks and other pagans anthropomorphised the gods, and ascribed to them human passions, and a corresponding morality; and made fate, and not free will, the supreme condition of moral existence, whether of gods or men. The attempt to explain the moral providence manifested in the course of nature and human life, resulted, by the natural recoil from the failure to solve the problem, with the Greeks, in bringing down the goodness of the gods to the human standard. The moral order and administration of the world seemed, to the Greeks, to rest rather on fate than on justice, on power than on right. And while the speculative reason of the pagan world, at best, but oscillated between fate and free will, its religious faith never rose above the enlightenment which rested its last hope for pardon of its shortcomings in this life, on the sacrifice of a cock to Æsculapius. A supreme God, as a moral governor of the world, was, at best, but an obscure sentiment in the background of the opinions of philosophers; and an individual immortality of the human soul, little else than a craving of their minds. They felt that, with their intellectual and moral instincts, they would not perish in the grave, but would live beyond it, in intellectual contemplation, as an assembly of philosophers. The grand moral fact, in the life of the pagan world, was, that the reason of man required of him more than he felt able to perform.

Though European civilization was born of Asiatic,

it had advanced so far beyond it in enlightenment, that Asiatic civilization seemed to have run its course in history, and to be only lingering in time to fulfil the condition of decay. The course of history, as if turning backwards, had carried European civilization into Asia, and the language of Greece had become in Asia a spoken tongue. European opinions had mingled with Asiatic, more in confusion than in conflict, creating rather doubt than enlightenment. At this crisis in human history, a person appeared at Jerusalem, who was born, in the humblest condition of life, in an obscure village of Judea, and proclaimed himself the light of the world, to show to man that way of life for which, under the sense of duty which is ineradicable from his nature, man had been seeking in vain by the light of his reason. He professed to have come into the world in a supernatural way, being born of a virgin, to fulfil prophecies that had for centuries been made by men of his particular race and nation, who claimed to have the foreknowledge of God given to them for the special instruction of the Jews. Moses, the chief of these prophets, had written, as he claimed, under the eye of God, a history of the creation of the world, just in the order of formation in which it was made; and had narrated how only one man and one woman had been made by God in his own image, to live in the world and to have dominion over it, and to people it with their children. He had stated, too, how this man and this woman had, of their free will, transgressed the commands of God, and thereby introduced sin and death into the world; and that it was one of God's ordinances that the sins of the parents were to be visited upon their children; and that thus it was that sin and death became the common heritage of the human family, all men having descended from the man and the woman who broke God's command. God had, according to this history, done the work of creation in six days, and rested on the seventh; and made it an example to man to labour six days, and to rest on the seventh for moral and religious improvement. So that, according to this history, the moral and religious government of the world rested on the two grand facts of creation, the work of six days and rest on the seventh, and the making one man and one woman the parents of the human family, and their transgression the cause of moral evil in the world.

Jesus Christ, as this man of Judea was called, at once recognized this account of creation and the fall of man into sin, as true, and declared that he had come into the world to fulfil the promise made by God, as told by the prophets, to deliver men from the woe that had been brought upon them by their first parents. He thus connected his work with the prime facts of the world. He so connected it with the origin of the physical universe and with the origin of man, in a moral filiation, as to be able to assume that it was part of the great scheme of administration which God had in his mind when he laid the foundations of the universe. The Mosaic history, which introduces the narrow Jewish polity, is thus made an introduction to universal history, with Christianity as the grand source of its moral life.

Moses, in his history of creation, gives, contrary to the universal doctrine of the pagan world, the only condition on which God can be thought to be omnipotent —*that matter is not eternal, but contingent;* and, therefore, it did not hamper God in his work of creation, as Plato and Aristotle taught, and thereby necessitate evil or imperfection. Neither did Moses, after the manner of philosophers, give any theoretical genesis of creation by formative forces of nature, but he merely narrated how the work was performed, in the order of its fabrication, by a personal God. And though Moses tells of God speaking to him face to face, as a man speaketh unto a friend; yet he also tells that God said to him, when he asked God to show him his glory, Thou canst not see my face; for there shall no man see me and live. This corresponds with the doctrine of God, which, as we have shown, speculative reason teaches. God can be manifested to man in finite relations, but not in his transcendent majesty.

Christ recognized as true the Mosaic representation of God, and offered no speculative solution of the great first cause. Neither did he after the manner of philosophers, propound any theodicy or metaphysical theory of sin, but pointed to the Mosaic history, as giving the true account of the fall of man; and offered, not a speculative, but a practical solution of the dreadful mystery. That justice, which made even the pagan world, in its conscience, feel that punishment must follow sin, is recognized by him as inexorable, and sinless as he claimed to be, he offered up himself to its behests, as a vicarious sacrifice in the stead of sinning men. He told men that God, of his free grace and love, as a compassionate father, had sent him, his only begotten Son, who is sinless, to suffer for their sins, and thus to leave them as free from guilt as if they had not sinned, if they would only accept the gift of grace, and become as little children.

The theism of nature, as well as the theophanies of the Jewish dispensation, is consummated in Christ. While, in the genesis of the notion of God, the manifestations of nature are, as we have shown, of deep import, leaving atheism without excuse, still, of God as the moral governor of the world, our best notions are derived from Christianity; for the moral character of God is too much obscured in the paradoxes of good and evil presented in nature and human life, ever to have been adequately discerned by human reason, as pagan philosophy shows. Neither could the peculiar theophany of Father, Son, and Spirit, consummated by the teachings of Christ, be inferred from nature. This conception of the Godhead gives vitality to the mediatorial scheme of Christianity, and solves, in a practical way, the moral paradoxes of the world. Whom the pagans ignorantly worshipped, Christianity professes to make known.

Christianity is, as it claims to be, in moral scope commensurate with the history of the world; and is interwoven in it, in many ways, as a guiding, formative, and educational principle.

Through the writings of Moses, which it adopts as true, and connects itself with, Christianity furnishes a clew to universal history. The materials for universal history, which the conquests of Alexander had opened to the European mind, from oriental sources, needed some central point which would present the nations of men as only different members of one common family. The Jewish Scriptures, which profess to be a compendium of the earliest history of the world, furnished this central point, in presenting families of men looking back to a past for a common origin, and forward to a future which determines them to a common destiny. In the beginning of the fourth century, after the appearance of Christ, Eusebius, Bishop of Cæsarea, arranged the facts of the pagan history, from the beginning of the Assyrian empire down to his own time, synchronously, side by side with those of the Jewish. And the Alexandrian antiquaries at once adopted the Scripture narrative, as the centre round which to group all they could find recorded of the oriental empires. But there was no certain basis for a valid chronology. It was, therefore, impossible to determine the proper order in time of either transactions or persons, or whether persons, bearing different names in Jewish history and in pagan, were different, or the same persons under different names, and other like difficulties. In the beginning of the sixteenth century, Joseph Scaliger took the Copernican astronomy as a basis for chronology.* From this he showed on what principles the ancient epochs and chronological systems had been formed. By this means he bridged the gulf between the classical and biblical worlds. He saw that the history of the ancient world could only, if at all, be known as a whole. The only materials for ascertaining the facts of the extra-classical ancient world, were the statements which the chronologers of the empire had copied and transmitted to succeeding times, without knowing their meaning. With the aid of the work of Eusebius, which he rescued from oblivion, Joseph Scaliger founded, upon the insight which the Copernican astronomy gave him into the chronology of ancient times, the basis of historical criticism which is fast unveiling the ancient pagan world to modern view, and proving

* Opus de Emendatione Temporum. By Joseph Justus Scaliger. Geneva, 1629.

by its success its own truth. The history of Moses and the astronomy of Copernicus are the two corner-stones on which historical criticism rests; the facts of the first, through the chronological clew furnished by the last, being rendered capable of being properly correlated with the facts of pagan ancient history; thereby giving us ancient history, both as to persons and transactions, as a whole distributed properly in time. The Jewish history, therefore, seems, by its relation to ancient pagan history, to have as strong evidence of its truth as the Copernican astronomy has of its truth in unravelling the chronological schemes of the pagan nations. They seem to be allied with each other, by that unity of truth which belongs to a consistent whole, whether that whole has the various complexity of a world, or is a more simple unity.

And Christianity, though originating at a period when a religion suited to all nations and peoples was thought by all to be impossible, and was opposed by Celsus on this ground, has fulfilled its high pretensions as a universal scheme of moral and religious culture, commensurate with the needs of men of all conditions and all times. It belongs to no one people, and to no one of the great geographical divisions of the historical life of the world. Though Asiatic in its origin, it has left Asiatic civilization behind it, and has become the prime formative moral influence in universal civilization. It rules all the relations of men, domestic, political, and international. By clothing itself, originally, in the Greek tongue, it has made all of Greek literature tributary to that broad culture, which the necessities of its polemics have introduced into the progress of learning. Its conflicts with error, necessarily, make it the chief exciting cause of learning and of speculative thought. That great Roman power, under whose imperial sway it originated in one of its obscure provinces, yielded to its influence; and the great body of civil law which that Roman power left, as its chief influence for good in modern civilization, owes its wiser adjustments of the reciprocal rights of social man, to the superior equities by which Christianity has tempered it in its applications to modern society. And the ameliorations of political government have been effected by the benevolent teachings of Christ. And that wider law of philanthropy, called international, of which pagan antiquity knew nothing, arose out of the broader doctrine of reciprocal right and duty, unbounded by race or nationality, which Christianity inaugurated. Even war has lost somewhat of its ferocity under the command to love our enemies. The deep insight into the fortunes of universal man, and the administrative forecast evinced, in conceiving and propounding a moral and religious scheme, which has proved so controlling for good, in general civilization, is altogether without parallel in history.

We have seen that the experience of the pagan

world was, that the reason of man required more of him, morally, than he felt himself able to perform. And this is the universal experience of men. Therefore, the moral faculty of man, which delivers, not theoretical, but practical judgments, is a mendacious faculty, on any scheme of morals and religion which does not embrace a vicarious element. Christianity makes, as we have seen, the vicarious principle the foundation of its scheme for reconciling sinning men to a just God. It therefore conforms to the moral constitution of man, and rescues his moral faculty from the paradox of commanding men to perform impossibilities—to lead a perfectly holy life. The moral command requires nothing less than perfect fulfilment. But the load of guilt is not lightened to man, because Christianity shows how he may be relieved of his burden; for the modern mind has, through the influence of Christianity in awakening the moral faculty to the evil of sin, come nearer to an adequate appreciation of human free agency and consequent responsibility. This is manifested, with extraordinary demonstration, in the drama of Shakspeare in contrast with the drama of the Greek poets. The remorse of Lady Macbeth, who is more conscious of her guilt than of a cruel destiny, in participating in the murder of her husband's guest, is in full contrast with the agonies of Clytemnestra, of whom we have spoken in illustration of the moral aspect of the Greek drama. Through the moral discriminations of human character, which Shakspeare borrowed from Christianity, he has portrayed the deep things of the spirit of man, with a fearful reality that the Greek dramatists never even approached. The moral life of an era is more perfectly exhibited in the drama than in any other species of literature.

But Christianity professes to be, not only a supplement to the light of nature which is the common heritage of all men, but also of the peculiar light which had been given, as a special gift, to the Jews. In this double aspect of a special complement to the narrowest and most exclusive of dispensations, and a supplement and consummation of the one catholic dispensation destroying the line of separation between men, which Judaism had established, Christianity is exceedingly remarkable. That a doctrine of the broadest charity and the utmost catholicity should grow out of the root of the narrowest exclusiveness, seems, to speculative reason, impossible. For the Jewish dispensation, if only a human institution, must be considered as the perfection of bigotry, and could by no analogy evinced in the history of human opinion, give birth to Christianity, which destroys its bigotry, and becomes the consummate flower of its root, to yield fruit not for Jews only, but for all mankind. But admitting that both the Jewish and the Christian dispensations are of divine origin, and do not belong to the ordinary course of historical development, then the mind moves more freely in understanding Christianity as a phenomenon in the history of man. Even if Christ had been a Greek, with all the liberal culture of Greece, so far are his doctrines above those of the Socratic, or any other Greek school, in purity and catholicity of morals, that he would have been a marvel; and the purity and sublime manliness of his character, coming up to the requirements of his perfect doctrine and to the terrible demands of his dreadful struggles with evil, would have exalted him as far above the Greek pantheon, as the grandeur of his death is above that of Socrates. The fishermen, who became his disciples, are as far before Plato and Aristotle in their importance in history, as these philosophers are before the fishermen in human learning and in speculative genius. Plato and Aristotle founded their moral scheme on reason, which promised to philosophers the felicity of intellectual contemplation in a future life. Christ founded his moral scheme on the affections, and made the dignity of life to depend on conduct, and promised to the ignorant as well as to the learned, the happiness of pure affections exercised on objects which impart peace and joy, not, however, in the darkness of ignorance, but amidst the light of intelligence.

As man is a moral being, knowing right and wrong, and yet prone to do wrong both from ignorance and an evil disposition, or an excess of passion, it is far more in accordance with speculative reason, to suppose that God would give him direct or supernatural instruction, than to leave him to the guidance of his own ignorance. The laws of physical nature, being bound in a necessity of undeviating antecedents and consequents, can be ascertained by human reason; and physical evil be thereby measurably avoided or prevented. But the moral code, except so far as it is founded on a narrow selfishness, never could, it seems to us, be discovered. The instincts of man would be taken by philosophers, as they were by Aristotle, as the affirmations of the moral rules for human conduct. But morality is, for the most part, a restraint upon these instincts, denying what they affirm; and in some instances deciding between opposite instincts; and at best, in all cases determining, as Aristotle did, the rule of rectitude by the result of good or evil consequences in the majority of instances. Morals are therefore objective and not subjective in their origin. They are an external rule, both restraining the instincts and directing them to their proper objects. The mind, thus having before it, as objective laws, a moral code like the Jewish decalogue, obeys it until, from the experienced adaptation of its precepts to the moral nature of man, it becomes the subjective law of every sentiment, word, and deed. There is no security for the purity and permanence of inward feeling, but outward law.

If there has been no revelation, and there certainly has been none, unless Christianity be such, man is without an authoritative moral code. Morals, then, rest upon the diverse opinions of different ages and of different peoples. Its sanction is only human. And yet it is the moral element of man's nature which constitutes his true nobility, and his relation to his Creator as the governor of the world. Take conscience from man, and he is, at once, only a higher order of brute. No responsibility, but that of fear of temporal loss, would attach to his conduct; and he need no longer perplex himself about a future state. For if man be not both a moral and religious being, conduct can have reference only to his physical welfare; and if he shall live in another state of existence, the violations of the laws of physiology will not extend their consequences beyond this life. Let man, if such be his nature, conform to the laws of hygiene, and he will enjoy all the felicity of which his constitution is capable. It is not possible for speculative reason to take this ignominious view of human nature.

From the foregoing considerations, according to every principle of rational conviction, we are shut in to the conclusion, that Christianity is a supernatural revelation; and that Christ was such an one as he represented himself to be.

We shall now enter upon considerations that will enable us to determine the relation of Christianity to human reason.

Christianity professes to be, not a product of human

reason, but a revelation of truths that are above reason. It does not ignore the light of nature, but supplements it; and does not give to human reason greater powers, but, recognizing its impotency and its limits, teaches a doctrine that is beyond the horizon of nature. Its voice is rather a whisper of consolation to that moral faculty, which sophistry, in all the long pilgrimage of pagan life, had not been able to pervert from its function of sovereignty over speculation on human duty, than a scheme of doctrines to satisfy human reason about the speculative difficulties which forced the great master of ancient philosophy to conjecture, that human reason is a wanderer in a strange region. Christ gave no solution of the moral paradoxes which result from the existence of evil in the world. He came to restore, reform, and regenerate, the moral kingdom of the world, by allying it more intimately with the kingdom of the future life. And in the prayer to the Father, which he gave as a model to his followers, the prime petition is, Thy kingdom come, Thy will be done on earth as it is done in heaven. The will of God, which is the supreme law, both in heaven and on earth, he came to make known as the rule for the guidance of men. We can know nothing more holy than the will of God. To set up any other rule of right, and justice, and truth, is both rebellion and irrationality. Unconditional obedience to the declared will of God is our duty. In our relations to

God our duties are absolute. They are imposed on us by a holy, omniscient, and omnipotent lawgiver, the stringency of whose decrees is not lessened by the opposition of either our wills or our reason. Rights and duties are not mutual correlatives in our relations to God. He has organized the world as it is according to his good pleasure; and has imposed a corresponding scheme of duties on man, which he must obey or suffer the penalty affixed to disobedience. Man cannot question the right of God to govern him, in his own way, without bringing down the absolute dominion of God to the level of the relative dominion of a human ruler. It was the duty of Abraham to obey God when he commanded him to slay his son Isaac. The freedom of man consists in doing the will of God. When Paul, in the Epistle to the Romans, discusses the paradox of the providence of God and the free agency of man, he does not propound any metaphysical theory of sin justifying the ways of God to human reason; but, recognizing the problem as insoluble, he rebukes the presumption of those who lay the fault of sin on God, the creator of sinning man, in these words, "Shall the thing formed say to him that formed it, Why hast thou made me thus?" Throughout all the discussions in this Epistle, of the great paradoxes of the moral world, the apostle in no instance, attempts, in his explanations, to solve a problem which lies beyond the limits of human thought; but he teaches the doctrine, in all its stringency, however contrary it may be to human reason in its conceptions of justice on the part of God towards man. That a doctrine is a stumbling-block or foolishness to human reason, has no force, with the apostle, against the Divine teaching. And as Christianity does not view this life as a sunny scene of Epicurean pleasures, but as an awful drama, in which the eternal fate of the actors is determined by the manner in which they act their respective parts, the relation of this life to eternity presents a problem which keeps the mind always on the border of speculation; and yet the apostles never betray an attempt, in their writings, to step over the limits of human thought. Mysteries are taught as mysteries, without any attempt at a rational criticism. And when a transcendental truth is enounced, it is done in a form wholly unspeculative; as, for example, Christ says, Before Abraham was, I am. Man must be humble in his ignorance, and obedient to the will of God. "It was (says Bacon) that ambitious and imperious appetite of moral science, judging of good and evil with the intent that man might revolt from God and govern himself, that was both the cause and means of the temptation, and gave occasion to the fall of man."

From the foregoing considerations, it is manifest, that in any attempt at a rational criticism of the positive articles of Christian doctrine, contradiction will emerge. Pierre Bayle, in the *Dictionnaire Historique et Critique*, formulized some of the contradictions which manifest themselves in a rational criticism of the articles of Christian faith, thereby, as he supposed, showing the irrationality of Christian faith. The contradictions he was unable to solve; and he oscillated, in restless skepticism, between the contradictions. In the article David, he attempted to show, that the moral perfection, called holiness, of revelation, was repugnant to our rational notions of morality, by assuming that the character of David was holy, and that therefore his acts, which to the human sense of morality were evil, were exemplifications of a holy character. As the assumption by Bayle is false, his inference of oppugnancy between morality and holiness, as standards of conduct, is a sheer sophistry. By a more cunningly devised paralogism, he exhibits, in the article Pyrrho, the contradictions between the doctrines of revelation and those of human reason, in the dogma of the fall of man, with the moral evils that are its consequences. "We ought," says Bayle, "to prevent evil when we can; therefore it is a crime if we do not when we can. Yet God does not prevent evil." Again, he says: "A person not in existence cannot be an accomplice in crime; yet original sin is a true doctrine." These difficulties, Bayle could not see, result from the constitution of the world admitting evil, and are not peculiar to Christianity. They only prove the impossibility of a demonstrative theology. Christianity assumes this impossibility; and therefore it was, that Christ came into the world to make known the way of life to man. "Woe unto the world," said Christ, "because of offences! for it must needs be that offences come, but woe to that man by whom the offence cometh." This declaration recognizes the inevitable existence of moral evil, but yet proclaims a woe against those who commit evil. Our not being able to understand why God does not prevent evil, neither invalidates Christianity, nor lessens the turpitude of sin. The declared will of God on moral subjects is the truth. And truth is the inevitable law of our thoughts, which we have no choice but to obey, by thinking it to be the truth. If Christianity is a divine revelation, we must believe its doctrines, whether repugnant to our reason or not; as repugnance to human reason, in transcendental truths, is because of the limits of human thought; and therefore, is no valid bar to faith in the supernatural, which Christianity claims to be.

These considerations bring us to the examination of the nature of that conviction, by which we believe in a revelation, called *faith*. The prime basis of all human intelligence is belief, called, plurally, primary beliefs. Knowledge, therefore, reposes on belief, and is only another name for belief when it is at its greatest certainty. Yet knowledge, in its turn, constrains to belief; and this secondary belief is sometimes, by writers, confounded with primary belief. What is meant by faith, is a secondary, and not a primary belief, and therefore it must be preceded by knowledge.

In the explication of faith, as thus defined, it is necessary to consider it in three relations; 1°. Its relation to knowledge; 2°. Its relation to reason; 3°. Its relation to its determining antecedents or objects.

1°. In its most limited meaning, knowledge is confined to self-consciousness and sensuous intuition. Any existence, therefore, beyond the limits of direct consciousness, can only be an object of belief, and not of knowledge in its most limited meaning. By this limitation of the meaning of knowledge, we cannot be said to know even the minds of our fellow-men, or that they have minds; for we are not directly conscious of them, but only infer, by belief, and not by deduction, their minds, from analogy to what we experience in self-consciousness. If we limit knowledge to this narrowness, we cannot be said to know God. And if we extend the meaning of knowledge, so as to take in the next step or degree in intelligence, and say that we know the minds of our fellow-men through analogy to our own minds, still, as we have not the same degree of intelligence of God as we have of man, if we confine knowledge to this degree, we cannot be said to know God. And the Scriptures recognize this difference of degree in our intelligence of man and of

God, in the remark, "He that loveth not his brother whom he has seen, how can he love God whom he hath not seen?" As, therefore, we infer by belief the minds of our fellow-men, we must be said to infer by belief, and from a less cogent analogy, the mind of God, or rather God himself, for to our intelligence God is only mind or spirit. But we know the attributes of God. We learn them first in ourselves, and ascribe them, by analogy to ourselves, to God. But we cannot know them in their infinity; for it involves an obvious contradiction to say, that we know the unfinishable in thought, which is the meaning of the infinite in its relation to knowledge, as our genesis of the notion, given in a previous part of this inquiry, proves, whatever may be its meaning in relation to existence, whether the unconditionally unlimited, or the unconditionally limited. But still the attributes which we know in ourselves, we only infer, by belief, to be in God; and therefore cannot be said to know them in God as by direct cognition.

In the acts of our intelligence in reference to objects, the form of conviction, in reference to a conceivable object, is different from the form of conviction, in reference to an inconceivable object. The first, in all the different degrees of certainty which we have distinguished in the preceding paragraph, is usually called knowledge, and the last is usually called faith. The last has its root in the first; as the inconceivable has its root in the conceivable; for it would be illegitimate to posit an inconceivable that is not some known reality thought of as infinite, such as space, time, or God, who is a personal reality thought of as infinite. Knowledge, therefore, constitutes the root, and furnishes the ground of the limits of belief in God, or of religious faith. It is through or because of knowledge, as defined in this paragraph, without distinguishing the different degrees of conviction in regard to the conceivable which we marked in the preceding paragraph. We can believe in the infinite and absolute only through the finite and relative. The boundary between knowledge and faith is irremovable and insuperable. For if man presumes to *know* what he can only *believe*, he is, at once, doomed, by the laws of his intellectual constitution, to equivocate forever between inexorable contradictions. But as soon as he humbles himself to the proper level of his intelligence, faith delivers him from the dilemma of contradiction, to the freedom of trusting to the teachings of Christ.

2°. But the relation of faith to reason is very different from its relation to knowledge. It presents the question, whether faith is a rational conviction or a mere blind passive feeling. In order to explicate faith in its relation to reason, we must consider three cases: 1°. I believe because it is consonant with reason; 2°. I believe although it is repugnant to reason; 3°. I believe because it is repugnant to reason.

In the first case, faith is so manifestly rational, that it needs no exposition to show it.

In the second case, reason makes a concession to faith. But as faith, as we have shown, is always founded on knowledge, there must be a foregone conviction to justify faith. In its weakness, faith, sometimes, because of something antagonistic to it in our reason, exclaims, "I believe, Lord help thou my unbelief."

In the third case, faith is put in entire antagonism to reason. Skeptics, in their attempts to invalidate faith in revelation, strive to show, that there is entire oppugnancy between faith and reason, as Bayle did. Revelation they say, must be believed not *although*, but *because*, it is in opposition to human reason. They exhibit, as the true formula of Christian faith, the extravagant purism uttered by Tertullian, in the *De Carne Christi*, when he said, "It is thoroughly credible *because* it is absurd"—"It is certain *because* it is impossible." While this paradox renounces all alliance with reason, and takes open opposition to it, its very form shows, that, though it ignores reason, it allies itself with reason, and depends upon it for its own validity; as the logical illation, expressed by *because*, demonstrates. The formula is therefore self-destructive; and can have no existence in human thought, except as a form of words veiling an absurdity.

The purity of faith does not require the divorce of faith from reason, as the extravagance of Tertullian implies, but only the adjustment of the relation between them. Faith does not rest upon the impotence of reason, but exists as a form of conviction in the human mind, because man is not omniscient. It is rather because of the limitation than the impotency of human reason. A want of confidence in reason within its proper sphere is not necessary to the strength of faith. But, on the contrary, the more potent reason is within its own sphere, the more certain must faith be within its sphere. The notion, therefore, that faith rests upon the infirmity of reason, and is strong in proportion as the infirmity is greater, is a sheer sophistry. The only plausibility it has, and that is not so much as a shadow of truth, is derived from the thought, that revelation is believed because of our confidence in the person proclaiming it. The thought has been expressed by Bacon in these words: "The more the divine mystery is contrary to reason, the more it must be believed for the honour of God."

We must acknowledge the supreme authority of the laws of thought over all human speculation, controlling all acts of our intelligent nature, not only those of the understanding proper, but of faith also. It is by recognizing the reality and universality of these laws, that faith is kept within its proper limits of rationality, and preserved from the paradox of Tertullian. For if the condition of non-contradiction is to be ignored in relation to the evidences of things not seen, and contradiction is to be no impediment to faith, then faith is the opposite of reason, and repugnance to reason is the criterion of credibility in divine things. And thus the *faith* of the philosophy of the conditioned, like the *reason* of the philosophy of the unconditioned, must repose upon the principle, that contradictories are one, and universal negativity the essence of thought in divine things.

3°. Faith, in its third relation, must be considered in several aspects, in order to explicate it; because of the different determining antecedents, varied as they are by circumstances of diverse logical positions.

The conviction, by which we believe in the infinite from our knowledge of the finite, is metaphysical or philosophical faith. By it we believe in an infinite God, from our knowledge of the physico-theological combined with the psychico-physiological proofs; as has been shown in the first part of this inquiry.

When revelation is considered as a scheme of transcendental truths, the relation of faith to it is not the same as to the transcendental in general as an abstraction. Our belief in revelation must, logically, rest upon our confidence in the person who makes it; whereas, in the metaphysical problem of belief in the transcendental as a generality, our faith is necessitated by the logical exigencies of thought. We must, therefore, discriminate between the basis of faith in the metaphysical problem of the transcendental, and the basis of faith in the problem of God and of revelation. In the abstract metaphysical problem, which is entirely logical and subjective, faith is determined solely by the relation of the finite to the infinite in human thought. But the relation of faith to the problem of God is determined by all those questions which we have discussed; and its relation to revelation is determined by all the questions which enter into Christian evidences. Whatever is transcendental in Christianity, all its mysteries, are, logically, believed upon miracle. Just as a man believes, against his unscientific reason, in the doctrine, that the earth revolves around the sun, because of the prediction of eclipses and of comets by astronomers, betokening an accurate knowledge of the mechanism of the heavens; so men believe, against their reason, which they feel not to be a complete measure of truth, in all the incomprehensible things in revelation, because of miracles performed by Christ and the apostles betokening superhuman knowledge. It has been argued, that miracles are impossible to human reason, because of the necessity to recognize, in our thinking, the order and uniformity of nature; and that, therefore, revelation cannot rest upon it for proof. But the order or uniformity of nature is only an empirical truth; and is not necessarily thought as an inevitable interpolation in our thinking about nature. It is only a reaffirmation that the same is the same, determined by the guidance of the law of identity. The objection, therefore, that miracle is impossible, as a valid human belief, falls to the ground. Hume's doctrine that a miracle cannot be proved by any amount of testimony, has long since, because of its often exposed invalidity, ceased seriously to vex theology.

With most Christians, however, faith rests upon the internal evidences, as they are called, the satisfaction which they experience in Christianity for their spiritual needs. This faith, which is more practical than speculative, is rather an intelligent feeling, founded upon an experienced adaptation of the doctrines to the human heart, than a conviction determined by ratiocination from external evidences. The aspirations and the needs of the soul are not unintelligent instincts, mere cravings after impossibilities, mendacious wants without any possible object of fruition in the universe; but they are a part of our spiritual constitution, and are as veracious deliverances of our intelligent nature, as the deductions of our reason, of which they are the handmaid, and often the guide. Reason or intellect, and the sentiments, are both elements of our intelligent nature, and in their proper union and logical adjustment, guide to the higher truths of the moral world.

The diversities of way, by which men are led to the gospel, are according to their native peculiarities and their previous habits of life. These, it is not within the scope of this inquiry, to explicate.

There must be, either an unconditional recognition or rejection of revelation. Any middle ground is impossible. The only criticism to which it can be subjected, must be founded upon its own resources. One doctrine may be compared with another, or one statement of the same doctrine with other statements, in order to clear up obscurities of meaning. And discoveries in physical science may be used in explanation of any statement of physical facts, such as the periods of time denoted by the six days of creation. The truth, that the world was created in successive phases, and peopled by successive creations of vegetables and animals, each perfect in its kind at the moment of its creation, and finishing the whole work with the creation of one man and one woman as the representative parents of the human family to be born of them, is not affected, in its moral bearing, by the discovery, that the periods, called days, are not mere rotations of the earth on its axis in twenty-four hours, but indefinite periods of time. The important truth is, that the world was created by instalments, in successive periods of time; and that the successive periods should afford a type, for a rule of conduct to man of labour for six days, and rest on the seventh for moral and religious improvement. The moral and not the scientific relation of a physical fact, is the intrinsic one in the statements of Scripture. The Scriptures do not teach science.

The doctrine of the limits of religious thought which we have presented as true, is substantially that maintained by Mr. Mansel* with such copious and apposite learning, such comprehensive thought, such dialectical vigour and subtlety, and such a pious spirit; though the course and aim of our argument is the reverse of his; ours being positive, and his negative. While we dissent from those critics who represent Mr. Mansel as making faith a mere feeling, only little else than the mute boundary of thought, still, both he and Sir William Hamilton push the doctrine of nescience further than we do. With all the acute discrimination of these two great thinkers, they both yield too much, it seems to us, to the Kantean distinction of *noumenon* and *phenomenon*. They, however, do not accept the subjective relativity of Kant, to the extent of making knowledge only a modification of mind, or a purely subjective product. They are both natural realists. The strong tendency of Mr. Mansel towards extreme subjectivism, is shown in his doctrine, that our conception of reality takes its rise in our minds through the intense consciousness of our real existence as persons. This one-sided doctrine cannot satisfy that dualism in thought, of subjective and objective reality, which is

* Limits of Religious Thought, etc. By Henry Longueville Mansel, B.D. Oxford, 1859.

the basis of natural realism. To thus make the notion of objective reality only the commutation of the subjective for the objective, as this doctrine seems to do, is at variance with any adequate doctrine of natural realism; and can only be maintained upon the Kantean doctrine of hypothetical realism, which must, in its ultimate logical reduction, end in absolute idealism. This extreme subjectivism and relativity taint Mr. Mansel's arguments more than his doctrine; his arguments being sometimes more negative than his doctrine seems to warrant. It was a negative purpose—to exhibit the limits of religious thought—that Mr. Mansel had; and it was next to impossible, in the argument at least, not to push the negation a little too far.

Though our knowledge is limited and relative, still it is true and real as far as it goes; truth consisting in the correspondence between our thought and the real thing thought about; the apparent being real, though not absolute, but partial and relative. The distinction between knowing a thing, only as it appears, and not as it is in itself, involves, to some extent, the ascription, to the human mind, of that mendacity which only the Kantean distinction of *phenomenon* and *noumenon*, and between the understanding and the reason, can support; and is a deception arising from the necessary existence, in all human or limited thought, of a general and a particular element, of the inseparable union and co-operation of conception and perception in all concrete thinking; conception referring to sameness or matter, and perception referring to diversity or qualities. This subjective dualism in thought, of conception and perception, is necessary to the knowledge of the objective dualism in objects, of matter and qualities. Matter and qualities are necessarily thought as mutual relatives; and they are just as inseparable in nature, and as completely one in real existence, as conception and perception are inseparable and one in actual thinking. That objects are really such as we apprehend them, is the doctrine of natural realism. We know this, it seems to us, or we know nothing. If we separate, in thought, matter and qualities, and endeavour to ascertain their mutual relations, we fail; and if we attempt to determine, in consciousness, the difference between them, we fail; for either, upon this last trial, will vanish as nothing, proving their inseparable unity, as an ultimate reality in nature, and an ultimate thought in consciousness. So, too, conception and perception are inseparable in their co-operation in actual thinking; each being impossible without the synchronous co-operation of the other. In human thought, there cannot be absolute unity; for the antithesis of consciousness is the highest and most perfect unity; and it is a dualism. The relativity of human thought necessitates this paradox of the one and the many, of identity and diversity, of matter and qualities; and limitation necessitates relativity.

From the limits of thought, Mr. Mansel determines, very justly, that philosophy has, within itself, no adequate criterion by which to test the validity or invalidity of the supernatural. It can, therefore, pronounce dogmatically neither for nor against a revelation. It can only prepare the way for the positive evidences of Christianity, by removing difficulties. This doctrine does not conflict with the argument, which we have presented in proof of Christianity as a divine revelation. Our argument is based on the relations of Christianity to the world and man.

We have thus given an outline of our views of the problem of God and Revelation; and we have exposed the futility of rationalism, while we have vindicated the rationality of faith.

With a view to the progress of philosophy in the future, consciousness may be discriminated into the understanding, the primary beliefs, the inductive belief or principle of philosophical presumption, the belief which guides thinking in the synthesis of effect and cause carrying our conviction beyond phenomena to an absolute creator, and the laws of thought.

We have shown, that the exposition of the laws of thought, in their relation to the condition of relativity, is a work yet to be done. Another important work to be done, is the determination of the true function in the mental economy, of the laws of association in their relation to the laws of thought. The adjustment, theoretically, of the mutual relation of these two sets of laws, would contribute greatly to correct thinking in the search after truth.

In presenting an outline of the progress of philosophy in the past, and indicating its future direction, we have, by our criticisms and suggestions of new doctrines, endeavoured to do something towards answering the demands of the present epoch so remarkable for earnest speculation.

THE END.

www.ingramcontent.com/pod-product-compliance
Lightning Source LLC
LaVergne TN
LVHW050516100826
845148LV00002B/358

* 9 7 8 1 4 2 5 5 2 1 3 2 5 *